CONTENTS

The oven temperatures in this book are for conventional ovens; if you have a fan-forced oven, decrease the temperature by 10-20 degrees. A measurement conversion chart appears on the back flap of this book.

ITALY

spaghetti bolognese

PREP + COOK TIME 2½ HOURS **SERVES** 6

2 teaspoons olive oil

6 slices pancetta (90g), chopped finely

1 large white onion (200g), chopped finely

1 medium carrot (120g), chopped finely

2 stalks celery (300g), trimmed, chopped finely

625g (1¼ pounds) minced (ground) beef

155g (5 ounces) chicken livers, trimmed, chopped finely

1 cup (250ml) milk

60g (2 ounces) butter

1½ cups (375ml) beef stock

1 cup (250ml) dry red wine

410g (13 ounces) canned tomato puree

2 tablespoons tomato paste

¼ cup finely chopped fresh flat-leaf parsley

750g (1½ pounds) fresh or dry spaghetti

½ cup (40g) shaved parmesan cheese

1 Heat oil in a large heavy-based frying pan over high heat; cook pancetta, stirring, until crisp. Add onion, carrot and celery; cook, stirring, until vegetables soften.

2 Add beef and liver to pan; cook, stirring, until beef changes colour. Stir in milk and butter; cook, stirring occasionally, until liquid reduces to about half.

3 Add stock, wine, puree and paste to pan; simmer, covered, stirring occasionally, 1 hour. Uncover; simmer, 1 hour. Remove from heat; stir in parsley. Season to taste.

4 Meanwhile, cook pasta in a large saucepan of boiling water until tender; drain.

5 Serve pasta topped with sauce and cheese; accompany with garlic or herbed bread, if you like.

tip Bolognese sauce is suitable to freeze.

serving suggestion A green leafy salad.

nutritional count per serving
▶ 26.6g total fat
▶ 13g saturated fat
▶ 2504kJ (599 cal)
▶ 41g carbohydrate
▶ 39.2g protein
▶ 5.5g fibre

minestrone

PREP + COOK TIME 4 HOURS (+ REFRIGERATION) **SERVES** 6

1 ham hock (1kg)

1 medium brown onion (150g), quartered

1 stalk celery (150g), trimmed, chopped coarsely

1 teaspoon black peppercorns

1 bay leaf

4 litres (16 cups) water

1 tablespoon olive oil

1 large carrot (180g), chopped finely

2 stalks celery (200g), extra, trimmed, chopped finely

3 cloves garlic, crushed

¼ cup (70g) tomato paste

2 large tomatoes (440g), chopped finely

1 small leek (200g), sliced thinly

1 cup (100g) small pasta shells

410g (13 ounces) canned white beans, rinsed, drained

½ cup coarsely chopped fresh flat-leaf parsley

½ cup coarsely chopped fresh basil

½ cup (40g) flaked parmesan cheese

1 Preheat oven to 220°C/425°F.

2 Roast ham hock and onion in a baking dish, uncovered, 30 minutes.

3 Place hock, onion, coarsely chopped celery, peppercorns, bay leaf and the water in a large saucepan; bring to the boil. Reduce heat; simmer, uncovered, 2 hours.

4 Remove hock from broth. Strain broth through a muslin-lined sieve or colander into a large heatproof bowl; discard solids. Allow broth to cool. Cover; refrigerate until cold.

5 Remove meat from hock; shred coarsely. Discard bone, fat and skin.

6 Meanwhile, heat oil in a large saucepan over high heat; cook carrot and finely chopped celery, stirring, 2 minutes. Add ham, garlic, paste and tomato; cook, stirring, 2 minutes.

7 Discard fat from surface of broth. Pour broth into a large measuring jug; add enough water to make 2 litres (8 cups). Add broth to pan; bring to the boil. Reduce heat; simmer, covered, 20 minutes.

8 Add leek, pasta and beans to pan; bring to the boil. Reduce heat; simmer, uncovered, until pasta is tender. Remove from heat; stir in herbs. Season to taste. Serve minestrone sprinkled with cheese; accompany with slices of crusty sourdough bread, if you like.

nutritional count per serving

▶ 7.2g total fat

▶ 2.4g saturated fat

▶ 865kJ (207 cal)

▶ 19.6g carbohydrate

▶ 12.7g protein

▶ 6.1g fibre

test kitchen tips

Use any small pasta in this recipe
such as macaroni, risoni or penne.
For information on washing leeks,
and baking and shredding ham
hocks, see page 112.

test kitchen tips

For a variation to the olives, fill the arancini with anchovies, tiny pieces of mozzarella or some finely chopped sun-dried tomatoes.

arancini

PREP + COOK TIME 1½ HOURS (+ COOLING) **MAKES** 24

2 cups (500ml) chicken stock

½ cup (125ml) dry white wine

45g (1½ ounces) butter

1 small brown onion (80g), chopped finely

1 clove garlic, crushed

1 cup (200g) arborio rice

⅓ cup (25g) finely grated parmesan cheese

⅓ cup (35g) coarsely grated mozzarella cheese

24 fetta-stuffed green olives (240g)

⅓ cup (35g) packaged breadcrumbs

vegetable oil, for deep-frying

1 Combine stock and wine in a medium saucepan; bring to the boil. Reduce heat; simmer, covered.
2 Meanwhile, melt butter in a medium saucepan over high heat; cook onion and garlic, stirring, until onion softens. Add rice; stir over medium heat until rice is coated in butter mixture.
3 Stir ½ cup of the simmering stock mixture into rice mixture; cook, stirring, over low heat until liquid is absorbed. Continue adding mixture, in ½-cup batches, stirring, until liquid is absorbed after each addition. Total cooking time should be about 35 minutes or until rice is tender. Stir in cheeses; season to taste. Cover; cool 30 minutes.
4 Roll rounded tablespoons of risotto mixture into balls; press an olive into the centre of each ball, roll to enclose. Coat risotto balls in breadcrumbs.
5 Heat oil in a large deep saucepan over medium-high heat; deep-fry risotto balls, in batches, until browned lightly. Drain on absorbent paper. Accompany with a rich tomato sauce for dipping, if you like.

nutritional count per ball
▶ 5.7g total fat
▶ 1.8g saturated fat
▶ 401kJ (96 cal)
▶ 8.1g carbohydrate
▶ 1.9g protein
▶ 1g fibre

seafood risotto

PREP + COOK TIME 1¼ HOURS SERVES 8

1.5 litres (6 cups) chicken stock

2 cups (500ml) water

2 tablespoons olive oil

1 medium leek (350g), sliced thinly

1 fresh small red thai (serrano) chilli, chopped finely

3 cups (600g) arborio rice

pinch saffron threads

1 cup (250ml) dry white wine

2 tablespoons tomato paste

1.5kg (3 pounds) marinara mix

1 cup (120g) frozen peas

2 teaspoons finely grated lemon rind

1 cup loosely packed fresh flat-leaf parsley leaves

1 Place stock and the water in a large saucepan; bring to the boil. Reduce heat; simmer, covered.
2 Heat oil in a large saucepan; cook leek and chilli, stirring, until leek softens. Add rice and saffron to pan; stir to coat rice in leek mixture. Add wine and paste; cook, stirring, until wine has almost evaporated. Stir in ½-cup simmering stock mixture; cook, stirring, over low heat until liquid is absorbed. Continue adding stock mixture in ½-cup batches, stirring until stock is absorbed after each addition. Total cooking time should be about 30 minutes.
3 Add marinara mix and peas; mix gently. Simmer, covered, 5 minutes. Uncover; simmer until all stock has been absorbed and seafood is tender. Stir in rind and parsley.

tip For information on washing leeks, see page 112.

nutritional count per serving
▶ 5.9g total fat
▶ 1.1g saturated fat
▶ 1547kJ (370 cal)
▶ 63.2g carbohydrate
▶ 8.9g protein
▶ 2.9g fibre

veal scaloppine

PREP + COOK TIME 30 MINUTES **SERVES** 4

8 veal schnitzels (800g)

¼ cup (35g) plain (all-purpose) flour

2 tablespoons olive oil

20g (¾ ounce) butter

2 tablespoons lemon juice

¼ cup (60ml) dry white wine

1 clove garlic, crushed

¾ cup (180ml) chicken stock

2 tablespoons rinsed, drained baby capers

¼ cup coarsely chopped fresh flat-leaf parsley

1 Coat veal in flour; shake off excess. Heat oil and butter in a large frying pan over medium heat; cook veal, in batches, until cooked as desired. Remove from pan; cover to keep warm.

2 Add juice, wine and garlic to pan; bring to the boil. Reduce heat; simmer, uncovered, until liquid is reduced by half. Add stock; simmer, uncovered, 5 minutes. Remove pan from heat; stir in capers and parsley. Season to taste.

3 Serve veal topped with sauce.

serving suggestion Mashed potato and roasted cherry truss tomatoes.

tip Veal schnitzel is thinly sliced steak available crumbed or plain (uncrumbed); we use plain schnitzel, also called escalopes, in this recipe.

nutritional count per serving
- ▶ 16.6g total fat
- ▶ 4.9g saturated fat
- ▶ 1572kJ (376 cal)
- ▶ 7.7g carbohydrate
- ▶ 46.3g protein
- ▶ 0.8g fibre

eggplant parmigiana

PREP + COOK TIME 1 HOUR SERVES 6

2 large eggplants (1kg)

olive oil, for shallow-frying

½ cup (75g) plain (all-purpose) flour

4 eggs, beaten lightly

2 cups (200g) packaged breadcrumbs

3 cups (750ml) bottled tomato pasta sauce

1 cup (100g) coarsely grated mozzarella

¼ cup (20g) finely grated parmesan

⅓ cup loosely packed fresh oregano leaves

1 Use a vegetable peeler to randomly peel strips of skin from eggplants (see page 112); discard strips of skin. Cut eggplants crossways into thin slices.

2 Add enough oil to a large frying pan to come 2cm (¾-inch) up the side of the pan; heat oil over medium-high heat. Coat eggplant in flour; shake off excess. Dip in egg, then in breadcrumbs (see page 112).

3 Preheat oven to 200°C/400°F. Oil 2.5-litre (10-cup) ovenproof dish.

4 Meanwhile, shallow-fry eggplant, in batches, on stove top, over high heat until browned lightly. Drain on absorbent paper.

5 Spread about one-third of the pasta sauce over base of dish. Top with about one-third of the eggplant, one-third of the cheeses and one-third of the oregano. Repeat layering. Season.

6 Bake parmigiana, covered, 20 minutes. Uncover; bake about 10 minutes or until browned lightly.

serving suggestion Rigatoni or penne pasta, or as a side dish to veal scaloppine.

nutritional count per serving
- 27.5g total fat
- 6.8g saturated fat
- 2257kJ (540 cal)
- 49.4g carbohydrate
- 19.9g protein
- 8.3g fibre

ricotta cheesecake

PREP + COOK TIME 1¾ HOURS (+ REFRIGERATION & COOLING) **SERVES** 16

90g (3 ounces) butter, softened

¼ cup (55g) caster (superfine) sugar

1 egg

1¼ cups (185g) plain (all-purpose) flour

¼ cup (35g) self-raising flour

RICOTTA FILLING

1kg (2 pounds) ricotta cheese

1 tablespoon finely grated lemon rind

¼ cup (60ml) lemon juice

1 cup (220g) caster (superfine) sugar

5 eggs

¼ cup (40g) sultanas

¼ cup (80g) finely chopped glacé fruit salad

1 Beat butter, sugar and egg in a small bowl with an electric mixer until combined. Stir in half the sifted flours, then work in remaining flour with your hand. Knead pastry on a floured surface until smooth; wrap in plastic, refrigerate 30 minutes.

2 Grease a closed 28cm (11¼-inch) springform pan. Press pastry over base of tin; prick with a fork. Place on an oven tray; refrigerate 30 minutes.

3 Preheat oven to 200°C/400°F.

4 Line pastry with baking paper, fill with dried beans or rice (see '*blind baking*', page 113); bake 10 minutes. Remove paper and beans; bake a further 15 minutes or until browned lightly. Cool.

5 Reduce oven temperature to 160°C/325°F.

6 Make ricotta filling by processing cheese, rind, juice, sugar and eggs until smooth. Stir in sultanas and glacé fruit. Pour filling into pan.

7 Bake cheesecake about 50 minutes. Cool in oven with door ajar. Refrigerate cheesecake 3 hours or overnight. Dust with sifted icing sugar before serving, if you like.

nutritional count per serving
- 13.8g total fat
- 8.2g saturated fat
- 1262kJ (302 cal)
- 33.2g carbohydrate
- 10.7g protein
- 0.7g fibre

test kitchen tips

Recipe can be made up to 3 days
ahead. Store, refrigerated, in an
airtight container.

FRANCE

boeuf bourguignon

PREP + COOK TIME 2¾ HOURS SERVES 6

280g (9 ounces) baby brown onions

2 tablespoons olive oil

2kg (4 pounds) gravy beef, trimmed, chopped coarsely

30g (1 ounce) butter

2 cloves garlic, crushed

4 rindless bacon slices (260g), chopped coarsely

400g (13 ounces) button mushrooms, halved

¼ cup (35g) plain (all-purpose) flour

1¼ cups (310ml) beef stock

2½ cups (625ml) dry red wine

2 bay leaves

2 sprigs fresh thyme

½ cup coarsely chopped fresh flat-leaf parsley

1 Peel onions, leaving root end intact so onion remains whole during cooking.
2 Heat oil in a large flameproof dish over high heat; cook beef, in batches, until browned. Remove from pan.
3 Add butter to dish; cook onions, garlic, bacon and mushrooms, stirring, until onions brown lightly.
4 Sprinkle flour over onion mixture; cook, stirring, until flour mixture thickens and bubbles. Gradually add stock and wine; stir over heat until mixture boils and thickens.
5 Return beef and any juices to dish, add bay leaves and thyme; bring to the boil. Reduce heat; simmer, covered, about 2 hours or until beef is tender, stirring every 30 minutes. Remove from heat; discard bay leaves. Stir in parsley. Season to taste.

serving suggestion Creamy polenta or mashed potato.

nutritional count per serving
▶ 31.4g total fat
▶ 12.1g saturated fat
▶ 2658kJ (636 cal)
▶ 6.6g carbohydrate
▶ 80.3g protein
▶ 2.8g fibre

test kitchen tips

For information on preparing the
boeuf bourguignon, see page 113.
Recipe is suitable to freeze.

french onion soup with gruyère croûtons

PREP + COOK TIME 1¼ HOURS SERVES 4

50g (1½ ounces) butter

4 large brown onions (800g), sliced thinly

¾ cup (180ml) dry white wine

3 cups (750ml) water

1 litre (4 cups) beef stock

1 bay leaf

1 tablespoon plain (all-purpose) flour

2 teaspoons fresh thyme leaves

GRUYÈRE CROÛTONS

1 small french bread stick (150g), cut into 2cm (¾-inch) slices

½ cup (60g) coarsely grated gruyère cheese

1 Melt butter in a large saucepan; cook onion, stirring occasionally, about 30 minutes or until caramelised.

2 Meanwhile, bring wine to the boil in a large saucepan. Stir in the water, stock and bay leaf; return to the boil. Remove from heat.

3 Stir flour into onion mixture; cook, stirring, 2 minutes. Gradually add hot broth mixture; cook, stirring, until mixture boils and thickens slightly. Reduce heat; simmer, uncovered, stirring occasionally, 20 minutes. Discard bay leaf; stir in half the thyme. Season with salt and pepper.

4 Meanwhile, make gruyère croûtons.

5 Serve bowls of soup topped with croûtons; sprinkle with remaining thyme.

GRUYÈRE CROÛTONS Preheat grill (broiler). Toast bread on one side then turn and sprinkle with cheese; grill croûtons until cheese melts and is browned lightly.

nutritional count per serving
- ▶ 16.7g total fat
- ▶ 10g saturated fat
- ▶ 1522kJ (364 cal)
- ▶ 31.1g carbohydrate
- ▶ 13.4g protein
- ▶ 3.9g fibre

quiche lorraine

PREP + COOK TIME 1½ HOURS (+ REFRIGERATION) SERVES 6

1 medium brown onion (150g), chopped finely

3 rindless bacon slices (195g), chopped finely

3 eggs

300ml (½ pint) pouring cream

½ cup (125ml) milk

¾ cup (120g) coarsely grated gruyère cheese

PASTRY

1¾ cups (260g) plain (all-purpose) flour

155g (5 ounces) cold butter, chopped coarsely

1 egg yolk

2 teaspoons lemon juice

½ cup (80ml) iced water, approximately

1 Make pastry.

2 Preheat oven to 200°C/400°F.

3 Roll pastry between sheets of baking paper large enough to line a deep 23cm (9¼-inch) loose-based flan pan. Lift pastry into pan; gently press pastry around side. Trim edge, place pan on oven tray. Cover pastry with baking paper; fill with dried beans or rice (see 'blind baking', page 113). Bake 10 minutes. Remove paper and beans; bake a further 10 minutes or until golden brown. Cool.

4 Reduce oven temperature to 180°C/350°F.

5 Cook onion and bacon in a heated oiled small frying pan, over high heat, until onion is soft; drain on absorbent paper, cool. Sprinkle bacon mixture over pastry case.

6 Whisk eggs in a medium bowl then whisk in cream, milk and cheese. Season. Pour mixture into pastry case.

7 Bake quiche about 35 minutes or until filling is set. Stand 5 minutes before removing from pan.

PASTRY Sift flour into a large bowl; rub in butter. Add egg yolk, juice and enough water to make ingredients just cling together. Knead gently on a floured surface until smooth. Cover; refrigerate 30 minutes.

serving suggestion A green leafy salad.

nutritional count per serving
▶ 51.8g total fat
▶ 35.4g saturated fat
▶ 3139kJ (751 cal)
▶ 35.4g carbohydrate
▶ 22.1g protein
▶ 2g fibre

nutritional count per serving

▶ 28.2g total fat

▶ 10.5g saturated fat

▶ 2750kJ (658 cal)

▶ 38.5g carbohydrate

▶ 55.8g protein

▶ 12.4g fibre

This is a traditional recipe from the Languedoc region in the south west of France, where the cassoulet is made from basic pantry ingredients that are always available. The many variations include duck or goose fat, with or without lamb, tomato, toulouse sausages or duck confit.

cassoulet

PREP + COOK TIME 3 HOURS (+ STANDING) SERVES 6

1½ cups (300g) dried white beans

300g (9½ ounces) boned pork belly, rind removed, sliced thinly

150g (4½-ounce) piece streaky bacon, rind removed, cut into 1cm (½-inch) pieces

800g (1½-pound) piece boned lamb shoulder, cut into 2.5cm (1-inch) pieces

1 large brown onion (200g), chopped finely

1 small leek (200g), sliced thinly

2 cloves garlic, crushed

3 sprigs fresh thyme

400g (12½ ounces) canned crushed tomatoes

2 dried bay leaves

1 cup (250ml) water

1 cup (250ml) chicken stock

2 cups (140g) stale breadcrumbs

⅓ cup coarsely chopped fresh flat-leaf parsley

1 Place beans in a medium bowl; cover with cold water, stand overnight. Drain beans, then rinse under cold water, drain. Cook beans in a medium saucepan of boiling water about 15 minutes or until tender; drain.

2 Preheat oven to 160°C/325°F.

3 Cook pork in a large flameproof dish, on the stove top, pressing down on pork with the back of a spoon until pork is browned; remove from dish. Cook bacon in the same dish, stirring, until crisp; remove from dish. Cook lamb, in batches, in the same dish, stirring, until browned. Remove from dish.

4 Cook onion, leek and garlic in same dish, stirring, until onion softens. Return meat to dish with thyme, tomatoes, bay leaves, the water, stock and beans; bring to the boil. Cover dish; transfer to oven. Cook cassoulet 45 minutes. Remove from oven, season to taste; sprinkle with combined breadcrumbs and parsley. Return cassoulet to oven; cook, uncovered, a further 45 minutes or until liquid is nearly absorbed and beans are tender.

tip For information on washing leeks, see page 112.

vegetable pithiviers with tomato sauce

PREP + COOK TIME 3 HOURS SERVES 4

10 large egg (roma) tomatoes (900g), quartered

2 teaspoons brown sugar

⅓ cup (80ml) olive oil

2 tablespoons red wine vinegar

2 large red capsicums (bell peppers) (700g), halved

30g (1 ounce) butter

2 large green zucchini (300g), sliced thinly

7 flat mushrooms (560g), sliced thinly

1 clove garlic, crushed

1 tablespoon port

5 sheets ready-rolled puff pastry

1 egg yolk

1 tablespoon milk

50g (1½ ounces) baby spinach leaves

1 Preheat oven to 180°C/350°F. Oil two oven trays.

2 To make tomato sauce: combine tomato, sugar, half the oil and half the vinegar in a large bowl. Place tomato pieces, skin-side down, on oven tray; roast 1¾ hours. Remove from oven; return to same bowl; crush with a potato masher, or a fork. Cover to keep warm.

3 Halve capsicums, place pieces, skin-side up, on oven tray. Roast in oven alongside tomatoes for about 40 minutes or until softened. Place capsicum in a plastic bag; close tightly, cool. Discard skin, seeds and membranes; slice thinly.

4 Meanwhile, melt butter in a large frying pan over medium-high heat; cook zucchini, stirring, about 5 minutes or until softened. Place zucchini in a small bowl; cover to keep warm. Cook mushrooms and garlic in the same pan, stirring, about 5 minutes or until mushrooms soften. Add port; cook, stirring, until liquid evaporates. Season.

5 Cut four pastry sheets into 16cm (6½-inch) squares; cut remaining sheet into quarters. Place one of the small quarters on an oven tray; centre a 9cm (3¾-inch) round cutter on pastry. Layer a quarter of the mushroom mixture, a quarter of the zucchini and a quarter of the capsicum on pastry (see page 112); remove cutter. Brush pastry border with combined egg yolk and milk; top with one of the large squares, press edges together to seal.

6 Using a sharp knife, cut around pithiviers, leaving a 5mm (¼-inch) border; mark the pastry with a swirl design from the centre to the side, without cutting through the pastry. Brush with egg mixture. Repeat with remaining pastry, vegetables and egg mixture. Bake pithiviers 25 minutes.

7 Combine spinach, remaining oil and remaining vinegar in a small bowl. Serve pithiviers with warm tomato sauce and spinach salad.

nutritional count per serving

▶ 74.3g total fat
▶ 10.5g saturated fat
▶ 4824kJ (1154 cal)
▶ 90.9g carbohydrate
▶ 23.5g protein
▶ 12.3g fibre

plum clafoutis

PREP + COOK TIME 1 HOUR (+ COOLING) SERVES 8

10 small plums (750g), halved, seeded

¼ cup (60ml) water

1 cinnamon stick, halved

¼ cup (55g) brown sugar

⅔ cup (160ml) milk

⅔ cup (160ml) pouring cream

1 teaspoon vanilla extract

4 eggs

½ cup (110g) caster (superfine) sugar

¼ cup (35g) plain (all-purpose) flour

1 Preheat oven to 200°C/400°F. Grease a shallow 2.5-litre (10-cup) ovenproof dish.

2 Place plums in a medium baking dish with the water and cinnamon; sprinkle with brown sugar. Bake about 15 minutes or until plums soften.

3 Remove cinnamon from dish and add to a medium saucepan with the milk, cream and extract; bring to the boil. Cool 15 minutes; remove cinnamon stick.

4 Whisk eggs and caster sugar in a medium bowl until light and frothy; whisk in flour then whisk mixture into cream mixture.

5 Place drained plums in a shallow ovenproof dish; pour cream mixture over plums.

6 Bake clafoutis about 30 minutes or until browned lightly. Serve dusted with icing sugar, if you like.

serving suggestion Double (thick) cream, custard or ice-cream.

nutritional count per serving
▶ 22.3g total fat
▶ 13.3g saturated fat
▶ 1526kJ (365 cal)
▶ 33.8g carbohydrate
▶ 7.5g protein
▶ 0g fibre

test kitchen tips

**This recipe is best made
on the day of serving.**

GREECE

spanakopita

PREP + COOK TIME 50 MINUTES MAKES 16

1.5kg (3 pounds) silver beet, trimmed

1 tablespoon olive oil

1 medium brown onion (150g), chopped finely

2 cloves garlic, crushed

1 teaspoon ground nutmeg

200g (6½ ounces) fetta, crumbled

1 tablespoon finely grated lemon rind

¼ cup each coarsely chopped fresh mint, dill and flat-leaf parsley

4 green onions (scallions), chopped finely

16 sheets fillo pastry

125g (4 ounces) butter, melted

2 teaspoons sesame seeds

1 Boil, steam or microwave silver beet until just wilted; drain. Squeeze out excess moisture; drain on absorbent paper. Chop silver beet coarsely; spread out on absorbent paper.

2 Heat oil in a small frying pan over high heat; cook brown onion and garlic, stirring, until onion is soft. Add nutmeg; cook, stirring, until fragrant. Combine onion mixture and silver beet in a large bowl with fetta, rind, herbs and green onion. Season.

3 Preheat oven to 180°C/350°F.

4 Brush one sheet of pastry with melted butter; fold lengthways into thirds, brushing with butter between each fold. Place a rounded tablespoon of silver beet mixture at the bottom of one narrow edge of the pastry sheet, leaving a 1cm (½-inch) border. Fold opposite corner of pastry diagonally across the filling to form a triangle; continue folding to end of pastry sheet, retaining triangular shape. Place on a lightly oiled oven tray, seam-side down; repeat with remaining ingredients.

5 Brush spanakopita with remaining butter; sprinkle with sesame seeds. Bake about 15 minutes or until browned lightly.

tip Uncooked spanakopita is suitable to freeze.

nutritional count per triangle
▶ 11.1g total fat
▶ 6.4g saturated fat
▶ 690kJ (165 cal)
▶ 11g carbohydrate
▶ 4.7g protein
▶ 1.5g fibre

dolmades

PREP + COOK TIME 3 HOURS (+ STANDING) SERVES 10

2 tablespoons olive oil

2 medium brown onions (300g), chopped finely

155g (5 ounces) lean minced (ground) lamb

¾ cup (150g) white long-grain rice

2 tablespoons pine nuts

½ cup finely chopped fresh flat-leaf parsley

2 tablespoons each finely chopped fresh dill and mint

2 tablespoons lemon juice

1 cup (250ml) water

500g (1 pound) preserved vine leaves

1 cup (250ml) water, extra

1 tablespoon lemon juice, extra

200g (6½ ounces) yoghurt

1 Heat oil in a large saucepan over high heat, add onion; cook, stirring, until softened. Add mince; cook, stirring, until mince is browned. Stir in rice and pine nuts. Add herbs, juice and the water. Bring to the boil; reduce heat, simmer, covered, 10 minutes or until water is absorbed and rice is partially cooked. Season; cool.

2 Rinse vine leaves in cold water. Drop leaves into a large saucepan of boiling water, in batches, for a few seconds, transfer to a colander; rinse under cold water, drain well.

3 Place a vine leaf, smooth-side down, on bench, trim large stem. Place a heaped teaspoon of rice mixture in centre. Fold stem end and sides over filling; roll up firmly. Line a medium heavy-based saucepan with a few vine leaves; place rolls, close together, seam-side down, on leaves.

4 Pour the extra water over top of rolls; cover rolls with any remaining vine leaves. Place a plate on top of the leaves to keep rolls under the water during cooking. Cover pan tightly, bring to the boil; reduce heat, simmer, over very low heat, 1½ hours. Remove from heat; stand, covered, about 2 hours or until all the liquid has been absorbed.

5 Serve dolmades with combined extra juice and yoghurt.

nutritional count per serving
▶ 7.6g total fat
▶ 1.6g saturated fat
▶ 690kJ (165 cal)
▶ 14.9g carbohydrate
▶ 7.7g protein
▶ 3.2g fibre

moussaka

PREP + COOK TIME 2 HOURS SERVES 6

¼ cup (60ml) olive oil

2 large eggplants (1kg), sliced thinly

1 large brown onion (200g), chopped finely

2 cloves garlic, crushed

1kg (2 pounds) minced (ground) lamb

410g (13 ounces) canned crushed tomatoes

½ cup (125ml) dry white wine

1 teaspoon ground cinnamon

¼ cup (20g) finely grated parmesan

WHITE SAUCE

75g (2½ ounces) butter

⅓ cup (50g) plain (all-purpose) flour

2 cups (500ml) milk

1 Heat oil in a large frying pan over medium heat; cook eggplant, in batches, until browned on both sides; drain on absorbent paper.

2 Cook onion and garlic in the same pan, stirring, until onion softens. Add mince; cook, stirring, until mince changes colour. Stir in tomatoes, wine and cinnamon; bring to the boil. Reduce heat; simmer, uncovered, about 30 minutes or until liquid has evaporated. Season.

3 Meanwhile, preheat oven to 180°C/350°F. Oil a shallow 2-litre (8-cup) rectangular baking dish.

4 Make white sauce.

5 Place one-third of the eggplant, overlapping slices slightly, in dish; spread half the meat sauce over eggplant. Repeat layering with another third of the eggplant, remaining meat sauce and remaining eggplant. Spread white sauce over top; sprinkle with cheese.

6 Bake moussaka about 40 minutes or until cheese browns lightly. Cover lightly; stand 10 minutes before serving.

WHITE SAUCE Melt butter in a medium saucepan, add flour; cook, stirring, until mixture bubbles and thickens. Gradually add milk; stir until mixture boils and thickens.

serving suggestion A greek salad.

tip This recipe is suitable to freeze.

nutritional count per serving
▶ 36.6g total fat
▶ 16.5g saturated fat
▶ 2420kJ (579 cal)
▶ 18g carbohydrate
▶ 41.8g protein
▶ 5.3g fibre

slow-roasted lamb with skordalia and potatoes

PREP + COOK TIME 5 HOURS (+ REFRIGERATION) SERVES 4

2kg (4 pounds) leg of lamb

2 cloves garlic, crushed

½ cup (125ml) lemon juice

2 tablespoons olive oil

1 tablespoon fresh oregano leaves

1 teaspoon fresh lemon thyme leaves

5 large potatoes (1.5kg), cut into 3cm (1¼-inch) cubes

1 tablespoon finely grated lemon rind

2 tablespoons lemon juice, extra

2 tablespoons olive oil, extra

1 teaspoon fresh lemon thyme leaves, extra

SKORDALIA

1 medium potato (200g), quartered

3 cloves garlic, crushed

1 tablespoon lemon juice

1 tablespoon white wine vinegar

2 tablespoons water

⅓ cup (80ml) olive oil

1 Combine lamb with garlic, juice, oil, oregano and thyme in a large bowl. Cover; refrigerate 3 hours or overnight.

2 Preheat oven to 160°C/325°F.

3 Place lamb in a large baking dish; season. Roast, uncovered, 4 hours.

4 Meanwhile, make skordalia.

5 Combine potatoes in a large bowl with rind and extra juice, extra oil and extra thyme. Season. Place potatoes, in a single layer, on oven tray. Roast potatoes for the last 30 minutes of lamb cooking time.

6 Remove lamb from oven; cover to keep warm.

7 Increase oven temperature to 220°C/425°F. Roast potatoes a further 20 minutes or until browned lightly and cooked through. Serve potatoes and lamb with skordalia; accompany with streamed green beans, if you like.

SKORDALIA Boil, steam or microwave potato until tender; drain. Push potato through a food mill or fine sieve into a medium bowl; cool 10 minutes. Whisk combined garlic, juice, vinegar and the water into potato. Gradually whisk in oil in a thin, steady stream; continue whisking until skordalia thickens. Stir in about a tablespoon of warm water if the skordalia is too thick. Season to taste.

tip Lamb shoulder can be used instead of a leg of lamb.

nutritional count per serving
▶ 57g total fat
▶ 14g saturated fat
▶ 4556kJ (1090 cal)
▶ 51.5g carbohydrate
▶ 91.2g protein
▶ 6.7g fibre

grilled haloumi

PREP + COOK TIME 10 MINUTES SERVES 6

500g (1 pound) haloumi cheese

2 tablespoons lemon juice

1 tablespoon chopped fresh flat-leaf parsley

1 Cut cheese into 1cm (½-inch) slices.
2 Cook cheese on a heated oiled flat plate (or in a frying pan) until browned both sides. Transfer cheese to a serving plate; drizzle with juice. Serve immediately, sprinkled with parsley.

tip Ensure that you eat grilled haloumi while it is still warm as it becomes tough and rubbery on cooling.

nutritional count per serving
▶ 14.3g total fat
▶ 9.2g saturated fat
▶ 861kJ (206 cal)
▶ 1.7g carbohydrate
▶ 17.8g protein
▶ 0g fibre

halva

PREP + COOK TIME 30 MINUTES SERVES 20

2 cups (440g) caster (superfine) sugar

1 litre (4 cups) water

2 cloves

1 cinnamon stick

220g (7 ounces) butter, chopped coarsely

2 cups (320g) semolina

½ cup (80g) coarsely chopped blanched almonds

2 teaspoons finely grated orange rind

½ cup (80g) coarsely chopped raisins

¼ cup (40g) blanched almonds, extra, toasted

1 teaspoon ground cinnamon

1 Grease a 20cm x 30cm (8-inch x 12-inch) slice pan or ovenproof dish; line base and sides with baking paper, extending paper 5cm (2 inches) over short sides.

2 Stir sugar, the water, cloves and cinnamon stick in a medium saucepan over medium-high heat until sugar dissolves. Bring to the boil; boil, uncovered, without stirring, 5 minutes. Cool 5 minutes.

3 Meanwhile, heat butter in a large saucepan until foaming. Add semolina and chopped nuts; cook, stirring, about 8 minutes or until browned lightly. Remove from heat. Carefully strain sugar syrup into semolina mixture (mixture will bubble up).

4 Return pan to heat, add rind and raisins; cook, stirring, about 1 minute or until thick and starting to come away from the side of the pan.

5 Spread semolina mixture into slice pan; top with extra nuts, cool. Sprinkle with ground cinnamon before cutting.

tip For information on toasting nuts, see page 113.

nutritional count per serving
▶ 12.4g total fat ▶ 36g carbohydrate
▶ 6g saturated fat ▶ 3g protein
▶ 1097kJ (262 cal) ▶ 1.3g fibre

BRITAIN

roasted chicken
with herb stuffing

PREP + COOK TIME 2¼ HOURS SERVES 4

1.5kg (3-pound) whole chicken

15g (½ ounce) butter, melted

HERB STUFFING

1½ cups (105g) stale breadcrumbs

1 stalk celery (150g), trimmed, chopped finely

1 small white onion (80g), chopped finely

2 teaspoons finely chopped fresh sage leaves

1 tablespoon finely chopped fresh flat-leaf parsley

1 egg, beaten lightly

30g (1 ounce) butter, melted

1 Preheat oven to 200°C/400°F.

2 Make herb stuffing.

3 Remove and discard any fat from chicken cavity. Fill cavity with stuffing, fold over skin to enclose stuffing; secure with toothpicks. Tie legs together with kitchen string.

4 Place chicken on rack over baking dish. Half-fill baking dish with water (water should not touch the chicken). Brush chicken with butter; roast 15 minutes.

5 Reduce oven temperature to 180°C/350°F. Bake chicken a further 1½ hours or until cooked through, basting occasionally with pan juices. Stand chicken 10 minutes before serving.

HERB STUFFING Combine ingredients in a medium bowl. Season.

serving suggestion Roasted pumpkin and parsnips.

nutritional count per serving
▶ 35.9g total fat
▶ 14.4g saturated fat
▶ 2437kJ (583 cal)
▶ 19.4g carbohydrate
▶ 45g protein
▶ 1.9g fibre

Split peas do not need to be soaked in water overnight. The relatively short cooking time produces a soup with more texture than usual.

pea and ham soup

PREP + COOK TIME 2¼ **HOURS** **SERVES** 6

1 medium brown onion (150g), chopped coarsely

2 stalks celery (300g), trimmed, chopped coarsely

2 bay leaves

1.5kg (3 pounds) ham hocks

2.5 litres (10 cups) water

1 teaspoon cracked black pepper

2 cups (375g) split green peas

1 Combine onion, celery, bay leaves, hocks, the water and pepper in a large saucepan; bring to the boil. Reduce heat; simmer, covered, about 1½ hours. Add peas; simmer, covered, 30 minutes or until peas are tender.

2 Remove hocks from pan. When cool enough to handle, remove meat from hocks; discard bones, fat and skin. Shred meat finely. Discard bay leaves. Cool soup 10 minutes.

3 Blend or process half the soup mixture, in batches, until smooth. Return to pan with remaining soup mixture and ham; stir soup over heat until hot. Accompany with crusty bread, if you like.

nutritional count per serving
► 4.9g total fat
► 1.4g saturated fat
► 1162kJ (278 cal)
► 31g carbohydrate
► 23.5g protein
► 7.3g fibre

roast beef with yorkshire pudding

PREP + COOK TIME 2¾ HOURS (+ REFRIGERATION & STANDING) SERVES 8

2kg (4 pounds) corner piece beef topside roast

2 cups (500ml) dry red wine

2 bay leaves

6 black peppercorns

¼ cup (70g) wholegrain mustard

4 cloves garlic, sliced

4 sprigs fresh thyme

1 medium brown onion (150g), chopped coarsely

2 medium carrots (240g), chopped coarsely

1 large leek (500g), chopped coarsely

2 stalks celery (300g), trimmed, chopped coarsely

2 tablespoons olive oil

YORKSHIRE PUDDINGS

1 cup (150g) plain (all-purpose) flour

2 eggs

½ cup (125ml) milk

½ cup (125ml) water

GRAVY

2 tablespoons plain (all-purpose) flour

1½ cups (375ml) beef stock

1 Combine beef, wine, bay leaves, peppercorns, mustard, garlic, thyme and onion in a large bowl. Cover; refrigerate 3 hours or overnight.

2 Preheat oven to 180°C/350°F.

3 Drain beef over a medium bowl; reserve 1 cup of the marinade. Combine carrot, leek and celery in a large baking dish, top with beef; brush beef with oil.

4 Roast beef, uncovered, about 1½ hours. Remove beef from dish, wrap in foil; stand 20 minutes before serving.

5 Increase oven temperature to 220°C/425°F.

6 Remove vegetables from dish with a slotted spoon; discard vegetables. Pour pan juices into a heatproof jug; stand 2 minutes. Reserve 1½ tablespoons oil from pan juices for yorkshire puddings, pour off remaining oil; reserve 2 tablespoons of the pan juices for gravy.

7 Make yorkshire puddings and gravy.

8 Serve beef with yorkshire puddings and gravy; accompany with roasted potatoes and steamed baby carrots, if you like.

YORKSHIRE PUDDINGS Sift flour into a medium bowl; whisk in combined eggs, milk and water all at once until smooth. Stand batter 30 minutes. Divide the reserved oil (from the pan juices) among eight holes of a 12-hole (⅓-cup/80ml) muffin pan; heat in oven for 2 minutes. Divide batter among pan holes (see page 112). Bake about 20 minutes or until yorkshire puddings are puffed and golden.

GRAVY Heat reserved pan juices in the same baking dish, add flour; cook, stirring, until browned. Gradually add stock and reserved marinade; cook, stirring, until mixture boils and thickens. Strain gravy into heatproof jug.

tip For information on washing leeks, see page 112.

nutritional count per serving
▶ 15.4g total fat
▶ 4.8g saturated fat
▶ 2169kJ (519 cal)
▶ 21.1g carbohydrate
▶ 61.2g protein
▶ 4g fibre

nutritional count per serving
▶ 20.1g total fat
▶ 11.2g saturated fat
▶ 1705kJ (408 cal)
▶ 47g carbohydrate
▶ 7.1g protein
▶ 1.6g fibre

classic trifle

PREP + COOK TIME 40 MINUTES (+ REFRIGERATION) **SERVES** 8

85g (3-ounce) packet raspberry jelly crystals

250g (8 ounces) sponge cake, cut into 3cm (1¼-inch) pieces

¼ cup (60ml) sweet sherry

¼ cup (30g) custard powder

¼ cup (55g) caster (superfine) sugar

½ teaspoon vanilla extract

1½ cups (375ml) milk

825g (26 ounces) canned sliced peaches, drained

300ml (½ pint) thickened (heavy) cream

2 tablespoons flaked almonds, toasted

1 Make jelly according to directions on packet; pour into a shallow container. Refrigerate about 20 minutes or until jelly is almost set.

2 Arrange cake in a 3-litre (12-cup) bowl; sprinkle with sherry.

3 Blend custard powder, sugar and extract with a little of the milk in a small saucepan; stir in remaining milk. Stir over heat until mixture boils and thickens. Cover surface of custard with plastic wrap; cool.

4 Pour jelly over cake; refrigerate 15 minutes. Top with peaches. Stir one-third of the cream into custard; pour over peaches.

5 Whip remaining cream; spread over custard, sprinkle with nuts. Refrigerate trifle for 3 hours or overnight.

tips The trifle can be made a day ahead. If they are in season, use sliced fresh peaches instead of the canned. For information on toasting nuts, see page 113.

test kitchen tips

Chelsea buns are best
made on the day of serving.
Recipe is suitable to freeze.
For information on toasting
nuts, see page 113.

nutritional count per bun
▶ 11.2g total fat
▶ 4.7g saturated)
▶ 1726kJ (413 cal)
▶ 70.3g carbohydrate
▶ 8g protein
▶ 2.7g fibre

chelsea buns

PREP + COOK TIME 1½ HOUR (+ STANDING) MAKES 12

4 teaspoons (14g) dry yeast

1 teaspoon caster (superfine) sugar

3 cups (560g) plain (all-purpose) flour

1½ cups (375ml) warm milk

½ teaspoon ground cinnamon

¼ teaspoon ground nutmeg

½ teaspoon mixed spice

2 teaspoons grated orange rind

1 tablespoon caster (superfine) sugar, extra

1 egg, beaten lightly

45g (1½ ounces) butter, melted

15g (½ ounce) butter, melted, extra

2 tablespoons raspberry jam

½ cup (75g) dried currants

¼ cup (55g) brown sugar

½ cup (60g) coarsely chopped toasted pecans

3 teaspoons warmed honey

COFFEE ICING

1½ cups (240g) icing (confectioners') sugar

15g (½ ounce) butter, melted

2 tablespoons warm milk

3 teaspoons instant coffee granules

1 Combine yeast, caster sugar, 1 tablespoon of the flour, and warm milk in a small bowl. Cover; stand in a warm place about 10 minutes or until frothy.

2 Combine remaining sifted flour, spices, rind and extra caster sugar in a large bowl, stir in egg, butter and yeast mixture; mix to a soft dough. Knead dough on a floured surface for about 10 minutes or until smooth and elastic. Place dough in a large greased bowl. Cover; stand in a warm place for about 1 hour or until doubled in size.

3 Grease two deep 22cm (9-inch) round cake pans.

4 Turn dough onto floured surface; knead 1 minute. Roll dough into a 23cm x 36cm (9-inch x 14½-inch) rectangle. Brush dough with extra butter, spread with jam. Sprinkle with combined currants, brown sugar and nuts, leaving a 2cm (1-inch) border all around.

5 Roll dough up firmly from long side like a swiss (jelly) roll. Cut dough evenly into 12 pieces; place six pieces, cut-side up, in each pan. Cover, stand in a warm place for about 30 minutes or until buns have risen slightly.

6 Meanwhile, preheat oven to 200°C/ 400°F.

7 Bake buns for about 30 minutes or until a golden brown colour.

8 Make coffee icing. Turn buns, top-side up, onto a wire rack. Brush hot buns with honey, drizzle with coffee icing; cool.

COFFEE ICING Sift icing sugar into a small bowl, stir in butter, milk and coffee until smooth.

MIDDLE-EAST

felafel

PREP + COOK TIME 1 HOUR (+ STANDING) MAKES 40

2 cups (400g) dried chickpeas (garbanzo beans)

1 medium brown onion (150g), chopped coarsely

2 cloves garlic, quartered

½ cup coarsely chopped fresh flat-leaf parsley

2 teaspoons ground coriander

1 teaspoon ground cumin

1 teaspoon bicarbonate of soda (baking soda)

2 tablespoons plain (all-purpose) flour

1 teaspoon salt

vegetable oil, for deep-frying

1 Place chickpeas in a large bowl, cover with cold water; stand overnight, drain.

2 Combine chickpeas, onion, garlic, parsley and spices in a large bowl. Blend or process chickpea mixture, in two batches, until almost smooth; return mixture to bowl.

3 Add soda, flour and salt to chickpea mixture; stir to combine, season. Stand 30 minutes.

4 Roll level tablespoons of mixture into balls; stand 10 minutes.

5 Deep-fry balls in hot oil, in batches, until golden brown. Drain on absorbent paper. Accompany felafel with hummus, baba ghanoush, tabbouleh and pitta bread, if you like.

nutritional count per felafel

▶ 1.1g total fat
▶ 0.1g saturated fat
▶ 100kJ (24 cal)
▶ 2.2g carbohydrate
▶ 0.9g protein
▶ 0.7g fibre

lamb kofta with yoghurt

PREP + COOK TIME 30 MINUTES SERVES 4

500g (1 pound) minced (ground) lamb

1 egg

1 small brown onion (80g), chopped finely

2 tablespoons finely chopped fresh flat-leaf parsley

1 clove garlic, crushed

2 teaspoons ground cinnamon

2 teaspoons sweet paprika

½ teaspoon cayenne pepper

½ cup (120g) yoghurt

1 Combine mince, egg, onion, parsley, garlic and spices in a medium bowl. Season.
2 Form lamb mixture into 16 sausage shapes; thread onto 16 small bamboo skewers or large, strong toothpicks, flatten slightly.
3 Cook on a heated oiled grill plate (or grill or grill pan) until browned and cooked as through. Serve with yoghurt, and accompany with lemon wedges and pitta bread, if you like.

tips Kofta can be prepared a day ahead; store, covered, in the refrigerator. Soak the bamboo skewers in cold water for 30 minutes to prevent them from scorching during cooking; or, for a faster option, wrap the ends in foil.

nutritional count per serving
- ▶ 10.8g total fat
- ▶ 5.6g carbohydrate
- ▶ 4.8g saturated fat
- ▶ 29.2g protein
- ▶ 1004kJ (240 cal)
- ▶ 0.4g fibre

tabbouleh

PREP + COOK TIME 30 MINUTES (+ REFRIGERATION) SERVES 4

¼ cup (40g) burghul

3 medium tomatoes (450g)

3 cups coarsely chopped fresh flat-leaf parsley

3 green onions (scallions), chopped finely

¼ cup coarsely chopped fresh mint

¼ cup (60ml) lemon juice

¼ cup (60ml) olive oil

1 Place burghul in a medium shallow bowl. Halve tomatoes, scoop pulp from tomato over burghul. Chop tomato flesh finely; spread over burghul. Cover; refrigerate 1 hour.
2 Add remaining ingredients to burghul mixture; toss gently to combine. Season to taste.

serving suggestion Lamb kofta or felafel, and accompany with pitta bread, if you like.

tip Burghul is made from whole wheat kernels, which are steamed, dried and toasted before cracking into several distinct sizes, so they develop a rich, nutty flavour. Because it is already partially cooked, burghul only requires minimal cooking. It is not the same as cracked wheat, which is raw whole wheat, and requires lengthy cooking.

nutritional count per serving
- 14.1g total fat
- 9.2g carbohydrate
- 2g saturated fat
- 3.4g protein
- 790kJ (189 cal)
- 5.6g fibre

chicken, spinach and cheese gözleme

PREP + COOK TIME 1½ HOURS MAKES 16

2 cups (300g) plain (all-purpose) flour

½ teaspoon salt

¾ cup (180ml) warm water

2 tablespoons olive oil

1 medium brown onion (150g), chopped finely

2 cloves garlic, crushed

2 teaspoons ground cumin

1 teaspoon ground cinnamon

200g (6½ ounces) spinach, trimmed

1 cup (160g) finely shredded barbecued chicken

125g (4 ounces) fetta cheese, crumbled

2 tablespoons lemon juice

1 Combine flour and salt in a medium bowl. Gradually stir in the water and mix to a soft dough. Knead on a floured surface for about 5 minutes or until smooth and elastic. Return to bowl; cover, while preparing filling.

2 To make filling: heat half the oil in a medium frying pan over high heat; cook onion and garlic, stirring, until onion softens. Add spices; cook, stirring, until fragrant. Transfer mixture to a medium heatproof bowl; cool.

3 Meanwhile, boil, steam or microwave spinach until wilted; rinse under cold water, drain. Squeeze out excess water; shred spinach finely. Stir spinach, chicken, cheese and juice into the onion mixture. Season to taste.

4 Divide dough in half; roll each piece on a floured surface into a 25cm x 35cm (10-inch x 14-inch) rectangle. Divide spinach filling across centre of each rectangle. Fold top and bottom edges of dough over filling; tuck in ends to enclose (see page 112).

5 Cook gözleme, both sides, on a heated oiled grill plate (or grill or grill pan), over low heat, brushing with remaining oil until browned lightly and heated through. Stand gözleme for 5 minutes before cutting each piece into eight slices.

tip You can replace the barbecued chicken with 160g (5 ounces) of cooked chicken mince, or use any leftover chicken you have handy – poached or roasted also work well.

nutritional count per slice
▶ 4.6g total fat
▶ 1.5g saturated fat
▶ 514kJ (123 cal)
▶ 14.2g carbohydrate
▶ 5.5g protein
▶ 1.1g fibre

nutritional count per piece
▶ 14.8g total fat
▶ 3.6g saturated fat
▶ 1124kJ (469 cal)
▶ 28.7g carbohydrate
▶ 5.4g protein
▶ 1.9g fibre

baklava

PREP + COOK TIME 50 MINUTES MAKES 16

1 cup (160g) blanched almonds

1 cup (140g) shelled pistachios

2 teaspoons ground cinnamon

1 teaspoon ground cloves

1 teaspoon ground nutmeg

18 sheets fillo pastry

75g (2½ ounces) butter, melted

ROSEWATER SYRUP

1 cup (250ml) water

1 cup (220g) caster (superfine) sugar

¼ cup (90g) honey

1 teaspoon rosewater

1 Preheat oven to 180°C/350°F. Grease a deep 22cm (9-inch) square cake pan.

2 Process nuts and spices until chopped finely; spread nut mixture onto an oven tray. Roast about 10 minutes or until browned lightly.

3 Increase oven temperature to 200°C/400°F.

4 Cut pastry sheets to fit base of pan; layer three pastry squares, brushing each with butter; place in pan, sprinkle with ⅓ cup of the nut mixture. Repeat layering with remaining pastry, butter and nut mixture, ending with pastry.

5 Using a sharp knife, cut baklava into quarters; cut each quarter in half on the diagonal, then cut each triangle in half.

6 Bake baklava 25 minutes. Reduce oven temperature to 150°C/300°F; bake a further 10 minutes.

7 Meanwhile, make rosewater syrup; pour hot syrup over hot baklava. Cool in pan. Accompany baklava with turkish coffee, if you like.

ROSEWATER SYRUP Stir ingredients in a small saucepan over high heat, without boiling, until sugar dissolves. Bring to the boil. Reduce heat; simmer syrup, uncovered, without stirring, for 5 minutes or until thickened slightly.

MOROCCO

mint and raisin couscous

PREP + COOK TIME 15 MINUTES **SERVES** 4

1 cup (200g) couscous

1 cup (250ml) boiling water

1 teaspoon ground cumin

½ cup (75g) raisins

2 tablespoons finely chopped preserved lemon rind

1 cup coarsely chopped fresh mint

¼ cup (60ml) lemon juice

1 Combine couscous with the water in a medium heatproof bowl, cover; stand about 5 minutes or until liquid is absorbed, fluffing mixture occasionally with fork.

2 Stir remaining ingredients into couscous. Season to taste.

tips Substitute 2 teaspoons finely grated lemon rind for the preserved lemon rind, if you prefer. Preserved lemon rind is a North African specialty; lemons are quartered and preserved in salt and lemon juice or water. To use, remove and discard pulp, squeeze juice from rind, rinse rind well, then slice thinly. It is sold by delicatessens, and is also available in jars from most major supermarkets; once opened, store in the refrigerator.

nutritional count per serving
▶ 0.7g total fat
▶ 0.1g saturated fat
▶ 1066kJ (255 cal)
▶ 52.8g carbohydrate
▶ 7.4g protein
▶ 2.5g fibre

spicy lentils with peas and potatoes

PREP + COOK TIME 40 MINUTES SERVES 4

2 tablespoons olive oil

2 medium potatoes (400g), chopped coarsely

1 medium red onion (170g), chopped finely

2 cloves garlic, crushed

1 tablespoon curry powder

2 cups (500ml) chicken consommé (or stock)

15g (½ ounce) butter

800g (26 ounces) canned brown lentils, rinsed, drained

2 red banana chillies (250g), seeded, chopped finely

100g (3½ ounces) baby spinach leaves, shredded finely

1 cup (120g) frozen peas

1 Heat oil in a large frying pan; cook potato, stirring, until browned lightly. Add onion, garlic and curry powder; cook, stirring, until onion softens.

2 Add consommé, butter, lentils, chilli and half the spinach to pan; bring to the boil. Reduce heat; simmer, uncovered, about 15 minutes or until potato is tender.

3 Stir in peas and remaining spinach; simmer, uncovered, until peas are hot. Season to taste.

tip You can substitute 2 cups (400g) dried brown lentils, soaked overnight and boiled until just tender, for the canned lentils, if you prefer.

nutritional count per serving
- 13.6g total fat
- 3.6g saturated fat
- 1271kJ (304 cal)
- 27.3g carbohydrate
- 13.4g protein
- 9.3g fibre

harira

PREP + COOK TIME 1¾ HOURS SERVES 4

½ cup (100g) french green lentils

500g (1 pound) diced lamb, cut into 1cm (½-inch) pieces

1 medium brown onion (150g), chopped finely

2 cloves garlic, crushed

1 teaspoon ground turmeric

½ teaspoon each ground cinnamon, ginger and hot paprika

pinch saffron threads

1.5 litres (6 cups) water

410g (13 ounces) canned chickpeas (garbanzo beans), rinsed, drained

½ cup (100g) white long-grain rice

3 egg (roma) tomatoes (180g), chopped finely

¼ cup finely chopped fresh flat-leaf parsley

1 Cook lentils, lamb, onion, garlic and spices in a large flameproof casserole dish, over high heat, stirring, until lamb is browned. Add the water; bring to the boil. Reduce heat; simmer, covered, 1 hour.

2 Add chickpeas, rice and tomato to dish; simmer, uncovered, about 20 minutes or until rice is just tender. Stir in parsley; season to taste.

nutritional count per serving
- ▶ 13.1g total fat
- ▶ 5.3g saturated fat
- ▶ 1919kJ (459 cal)
- ▶ 41.4g carbohydrate
- ▶ 39.1g protein
- ▶ 8.3g fibre

nutritional count per serving
▶ 25.7g total fat
▶ 7.5g saturated fat
▶ 2023kJ (484 cal)
▶ 16.9g carbohydrate
▶ 44.2g protein
▶ 4.7g fibre

Ras el hanout is a Moroccan spice mixture meaning 'top of the shelf'. The mixture varies from one merchant to another, but is always subtly savoury with a touch of heat.

lamb tagine with ras el hanout

PREP + COOK TIME 1 HOUR (+ REFRIGERATION) SERVES 4

750g (1½ pounds) boned lamb shoulder, chopped coarsely

2 tablespoons ras el hanout

¼ cup (60ml) olive oil

8 baby new (chat) potatoes (320g), halved

2 small leeks (400g), sliced thinly

1 litre (4 cups) beef consommé (or stock)

2 tablespoons finely chopped fresh flat-leaf parsley

1 Combine lamb, ras el hanout and 1 tablespoon of the oil in a large bowl. Cover, refrigerate lamb for 3 hours or overnight.

2 Preheat oven to 200°C/400°F.

3 Heat 1 tablespoon of the remaining oil in a tagine or flameproof casserole dish on the stove top over high heat; cook lamb, in batches, until browned. Remove from tagine.

4 Heat remaining oil in the same tagine; cook potato and leek, stirring, until potatoes are browned lightly and leek softens. Return lamb to tagine with consommé; bring to the boil.

5 Cover tagine, transfer to oven; cook 45 minutes or until lamb is tender. Remove from oven; stir in parsley, season to taste.

tip For information on washing leeks, see page 112.

M'hanncha means 'the snake'
and this coiled sweet pastry treat
certainly represents that.

m'hanncha

PREP + COOK TIME 55 MINUTES **SERVES** 8

90g (3 ounces) butter, melted

1⅔ cups (200g) ground almonds

½ teaspoon almond essence

½ cup (80g) icing (confectioners') sugar

2 teaspoons rosewater

45g (1½ ounces) dark (semi-sweet) chocolate, grated coarsely

6 sheets fillo pastry

75g (2½ ounces) butter, extra, melted

1 egg, beaten lightly

½ teaspoon ground cinnamon

1 Preheat oven to 160°C/325°F. Grease a closed 20cm (8-inch) springform tin.

2 Combine butter, ground almonds, essence, sifted icing sugar, rosewater and chocolate in a medium bowl. Roll rounded teaspoons of mixture into balls. Roll balls into 2.5cm (1-inch) log shapes.

3 Brush 1 sheet of pastry with some of the extra butter; top with a second pastry sheet, brush with butter. Place one-third of the chocolate logs along one long end of the pastry, 5cm (2-inches) from edge, leaving a 2.5cm (1-inch) border on short ends. Roll pastry tightly to enclose logs. Repeat with remaining pastry, butter and logs. Brush pastry logs with butter.

4 Pinch one end of one pastry log to seal – this will become the centre of the spiral. Wind the pastry log into a tight spiral, brushing with egg to join. Continue adding pastry logs, end-to-end, in a spiral pattern, brushing with egg to join and seal ends. Transfer spiral to tin. Brush with egg, sprinkle with cinnamon. Bake about 25 minutes or until golden.

5 Serve dusted with a little sifted icing sugar.

nutritional count per serving
▶ 33.3g total fat
▶ 13.3g saturated fat
▶ 1710kJ (409 cal)
▶ 20.5g carbohydrate
▶ 7.4g protein
▶ 2.5g fibre

INDIA

rogan josh

PREP + COOK TIME 2½ HOURS SERVES 4

1kg (2 pounds) boned leg of lamb, trimmed, diced into 3cm (1¼-inch) pieces

2 teaspoons each ground cardamom, cumin and coriander

20g (¾ ounce) butter

2 tablespoons vegetable oil

2 medium brown onions (300g), sliced thinly

4cm (1½-inch) piece fresh ginger (20g), grated

4 cloves garlic, crushed

2 teaspoons sweet paprika

½ teaspoon cayenne pepper

½ cup (125ml) beef stock

410g (13 ounces) canned crushed tomatoes

2 bay leaves

2 cinnamon sticks

200g (6½ ounces) yoghurt

¾ cup (110g) toasted slivered almonds

1 fresh long red chilli, sliced thinly

RAITA

1 cup (280g) thick yoghurt

1 lebanese cucumber (130g), seeded, chopped finely

1 tablespoon finely chopped fresh mint

pinch ground cumin

1 Combine lamb and ground cardamom, cumin and coriander in a medium bowl.

2 Heat butter and half the oil in a large deep saucepan over high heat; cook lamb, in batches, until browned all over. Remove from pan.

3 Heat remaining oil in the same pan; cook onion, ginger, garlic, paprika and cayenne, over low heat, stirring, until onion softens.

4 Return lamb to pan with stock, tomatoes, bay leaves and cinnamon. Add yoghurt, 1 tablespoon at a time, stirring well between each addition; bring to the boil. Reduce heat; simmer, covered, about 1½ hours or until lamb is tender.

5 Meanwhile, make raita.

6 Remove lamb from the heat; sprinkle lamb with nuts and chilli. Serve with raita, and warmed naan bread, if you like.

RAITA Combine ingredients in a small bowl; season to taste.

serving suggestion Steamed basmati rice.

nutritional count per serving
▶ 48.1g total fat
▶ 15.3g saturated fat
▶ 3219kJ (770 cal)
▶ 15.7g carbohydrate
▶ 68.9g protein
▶ 5.5g fibre

beef samosas with peach and raisin chutney

PREP + COOK TIME 2¼ HOURS (+ REFRIGERATION) **MAKES** 36

2 teaspoons vegetable oil

1 small brown onion (80g), chopped finely

2 cloves garlic, crushed

2cm (¾-inch) piece fresh ginger (10g), grated

1 tablespoon each ground cumin and coriander

1 fresh small red thai (serrano) chilli, chopped finely

250g (8 ounces) minced (ground) beef

1 small kumara (orange sweet potato) (250g), chopped finely

⅓ cup (80ml) water

4 sheets shortcrust pastry

1 egg, beaten lightly

PEACH AND RAISIN CHUTNEY

3 medium peaches (450g)

1 small brown onion (80g), chopped finely

⅓ cup (110g) raisins, chopped finely

½ cup (125ml) apple cider vinegar

2 tablespoons lemon juice

1 cup (220g) white sugar

½ teaspoon ground allspice

¼ teaspoon ground cinnamon

1 Make peach and raisin chutney.

2 Heat oil in a large frying pan; cook onion, garlic, ginger and spices, stirring, until onion softens. Add chilli and mince; cook, stirring, until mince browns. Add kumara and the water; bring to the boil. Reduce heat; simmer, uncovered, stirring occasionally, until kumara softens. Stir in ⅓ cup of the chutney; season. Cool filling 10 minutes then refrigerate until cold.

3 Preheat oven to 200°C/400°F. Oil 3 oven trays.

4 Using a 7.5cm (3-inch) round cutter, cut nine rounds from each pastry sheet. Place rounded teaspoons of the beef filling in the centre of each round; brush edge of round with egg, press edges together to enclose filling. Repeat process with remaining rounds and filling. Place samosas on oven trays; brush tops with any remaining egg. Bake, uncovered, about 20 minutes or until samosas are browned lightly.

PEACH AND RAISIN CHUTNEY Cover peaches with boiling water in a medium heatproof bowl for about 30 seconds. Peel, seed, then chop peaches finely. Place chopped flesh in a medium saucepan with remaining ingredients; bring to the boil. Reduce heat; simmer, uncovered, stirring occasionally, about 45 minutes or until chutney thickens (add a small amount of water to chutney, if necessary).

tip Chutney can be made a week ahead; store in a sterilised jar, in the refrigerator. For information on sterilising jars, see glossary, page 116.

nutritional count per samosa
▶ 5.7g total fat
▶ 2.8g saturated fat
▶ 560 kJ (134 cal)
▶ 17.8g carbohydrate
▶ 3.1g protein
▶ 0.8g fibre

lamb biryani

PREP + COOK TIME 2¾ HOURS (+ REFRIGERATION) **SERVES** 4

1kg (2 pounds) lamb shoulder, cut into 3cm (1¼-inch) pieces

3cm (1¼-inch) piece fresh ginger (15g), grated

2 cloves garlic, crushed

2 fresh small red thai (serrano) chillies, chopped finely

2 teaspoons garam masala

1 tablespoon finely chopped fresh coriander (cilantro)

¼ teaspoon ground turmeric

½ cup (140g) yoghurt

2 tablespoons ghee

½ cup (40g) flaked almonds

¼ cup (40g) sultanas

2 medium brown onions (300g), sliced thickly

½ cup (125ml) water

pinch saffron threads

1 tablespoon hot milk

1½ cups (300g) basmati rice

¼ cup firmly packed fresh coriander leaves (cilantro)

1 Combine lamb, ginger, garlic, chilli, garam masala, chopped coriander, turmeric and yoghurt in a medium bowl. Cover; refrigerate lamb overnight.

2 Heat half the ghee in a large saucepan; cook nuts and sultanas, stirring, until nuts brown lightly. Remove from pan.

3 Heat remaining ghee in the same pan; cook onion, covered, for 5 minutes. Uncover; cook, stirring occasionally, about 5 minutes or until browned lightly. Reserve half the onion.

4 Add lamb mixture to pan; cook, stirring, until browned. Add the water; bring to the boil. Reduce heat; simmer, covered, 1 hour. Uncover; simmer about 30 minutes or until lamb is tender and sauce is thickened.

5 Meanwhile, combine saffron and milk in a small bowl; stand 15 minutes.

6 Cook rice in a medium saucepan of boiling water, uncovered, for 5 minutes; drain.

7 Preheat oven to 180°C/350°F.

8 Spread half the lamb mixture into an oiled deep 2-litre (8-cup) ovenproof dish. Layer with half the rice; top with remaining lamb mixture then remaining rice. Drizzle milk mixture over rice; cover tightly with greased foil and lid (or two layers of foil). Bake about 30 minutes or until rice is tender.

9 Serve biryani topped with reserved onion, nut and sultana mixture, and coriander leaves.

nutritional count per serving
- ▶ 38.6g total fat
- ▶ 17.4g saturated fat
- ▶ 3703kJ (886 cal)
- ▶ 73.8g carbohydrate
- ▶ 58.7g protein
- ▶ 3.4g fibre

nutritional count per serving
- ▶ 4.6g total fat
- ▶ 1.1g saturated fat
- ▶ 1308kJ (313 cal)
- ▶ 53.4g carbohydrate
- ▶ 14g protein
- ▶ 10.2g fibre

masala dosa with mint rasam

PREP + COOK TIME 55 MINUTES SERVES 4

2 large potatoes (600g), cut into 2cm
(¾-inch) pieces

1 tablespoon dried chickpeas (garbanzo beans)

2 teaspoons vegetable oil

2 medium brown onions (300g), sliced thinly

1 teaspoon black mustard seeds

½ teaspoon dried chilli flakes

1 teaspoon ground turmeric

10 dried curry leaves

¾ cup (180ml) buttermilk

2 tablespoons finely chopped fresh coriander
(cilantro)

4 chapatis

¼ cup (80g) mango chutney

MINT RASAM

2 teaspoons red lentils

2 teaspoons coriander seeds

½ teaspoon cumin seeds

½ teaspoon dried chilli flakes

2 medium tomatoes (300g), chopped coarsely

1 long green chilli, chopped finely

1 cup coarsely chopped fresh mint

¼ cup (50g) red lentils, extra

1 tablespoon tamarind paste

1¼ cups (310ml) water

1 Boil, steam or microwave potato until tender;
drain.

2 Meanwhile, using mortar and pestle, lightly
crush chickpeas.

3 Heat oil in a large frying pan over high heat;
cook onion, stirring, until soft. Add seeds, chilli,
turmeric, curry leaves and crushed chickpeas;
cook, stirring occasionally, over medium heat,
for 10 minutes. Add potato and buttermilk; cook,
covered, over low heat, for 5 minutes. Stir in
coriander; season to taste.

4 Meanwhile, make mint rasam.

5 Warm chapatis, one at a time, in a large
heated frying pan, over medium heat; place a
quarter of the potato masala on each chapati
then roll into a cone shape. Serve with mint
rasam and chutney.

MINT RASAM Dry-fry lentils, seeds and
chilli flakes in a small frying pan, stirring,
until fragrant. Using a mortar and pestle,
crush mixture finely. Place tomato, green chilli,
mint and lentil mixture in a medium saucepan;
cook, stirring, for 5 minutes. Add extra lentils,
tamarind and the water; bring to the boil.
Boil, uncovered, stirring occasionally, about
10 minutes or until lentils are soft and liquid
has almost evaporated.

**tip You can lightly crush chickpeas and
dry-fried lentil mixture in a spice grinder
or food processor.**

tandoori chicken

PREP + COOK TIME 2 HOURS (+ REFRIGERATION) **SERVES** 6

½ cup (150g) tandoori paste

1 cup (280g) yoghurt

2 cloves garlic, crushed

2cm (¾-inch) piece fresh ginger (10g), chopped coarsely

1.6kg (3¼-pound) whole chicken

1 cup (250ml) green ginger wine

1 Combine paste, yoghurt, garlic and ginger in a large bowl; add chicken. Rub tandoori mixture all over chicken. Cover; refrigerate overnight.

2 Preheat oven to 180°C/350°F.

3 Tuck chicken wings under body; tie legs together with kitchen string. Place chicken on an oiled rack over baking dish. Pour wine into baking dish; bake about 1½ hours or until chicken is cooked through.

serving suggestion Coriander, cucumber and mint salad and mint raita.

nutritional count per serving
- 18.3g total fat
- 5.3g saturated fat
- 2031kJ (486 cal)
- 9.1g carbohydrate
- 61.4g protein
- 0.3g fibre

pistachio, honey and cardamom kulfi

PREP + COOK TIME 25 MINUTES (+ COOLING & FREEZING) **SERVES** 4

2 x 375ml (12 ounces) cans evaporated milk

¾ cup (180ml) pouring cream

3 cardamom pods, bruised

2 tablespoons honey

⅓ cup (45g) finely chopped toasted pistachios

2 tablespoons coarsely chopped toasted pistachios, extra

1 Bring milk, cream and cardamom to the boil in a large heavy-based saucepan. Reduce heat; simmer, uncovered, stirring occasionally, about 10 minutes or until reduced to about 3 cups. Stir in honey, remove from heat; cool 15 minutes.

2 Strain mixture into a large bowl; discard cardamom. Divide kulfi mixture among 4 x ¾-cup (180ml) moulds; sprinkle with finely chopped nuts. Cover with foil; freeze 3 hours or overnight.

3 Turn kulfi onto serving plates; sprinkle with coarsely chopped nuts to serve.

nutritional count per serving
- 45.1g total fat
- 36.3g carbohydrate
- 25.6g saturated fat
- 19.3g protein
- 2621kJ (627 cal)
- 1.7g fibre

73

ASIA

beef rendang

PREP + COOK TIME 2¼ HOURS SERVES 6

1.5kg (3 pounds) beef chuck steak, trimmed, cut into 3cm (1¼-inch) cubes

410ml (13 ounces) canned coconut milk

½ cup (125ml) water

10cm (4-inch) stick fresh lemon grass (20g), bruised

3 fresh kaffir lime leaves, torn

SPICE PASTE

2 medium red onions (340g), chopped coarsely

4 cloves garlic, chopped coarsely

5cm (2-inch) piece fresh ginger (25g), chopped

2 fresh long red chillies, chopped coarsely

3 teaspoons grated fresh galangal

3 teaspoons ground coriander

1½ teaspoons ground cumin

1 teaspoon ground turmeric

1 teaspoon salt

1 Make spice paste.

2 Combine paste in wok with beef, coconut milk, the water, lemon grass and lime leaves; bring to the boil. Reduce heat; simmer, covered, stirring occasionally, about 2 hours or until mixture thickens and beef is tender.

SPICE PASTE Blend or process ingredients into a paste.

serving suggestion Steamed rice.

test kitchen tips

Recipe can made a day ahead; store, covered, in the refrigerator — this allows the flavours to develop overnight.

nutritional count per serving
▶ 25.2g total fat
▶ 16.9g saturated fat
▶ 1952kJ (467 cal)
▶ 6.1g carbohydrate
▶ 52.9g protein
▶ 2.5g fibre

tom kha gai

PREP + COOK TIME 45 MINUTES **SERVES** 12

250g (8 ounces) chicken tenderloins

1½ cups (375ml) water

1½ cups (375ml) chicken stock

410ml (13 ounces) canned coconut milk

2cm (¾-inch) piece fresh ginger (10g), peeled, sliced thinly

10cm (4-inch) stick fresh lemon grass (20g), bruised

4 fresh kaffir lime leaves, torn

1 fresh small red thai (serrano) chilli, halved lengthways

¼ cup finely chopped fresh coriander (cilantro) root

2 teaspoons fish sauce

1 teaspoon grated palm sugar

1 tablespoon lime juice

45g (1½ ounces) straw mushrooms, sliced thinly

3 fresh kaffir lime leaves, extra, shredded finely

2 fresh small red thai (serrano) chillies, extra, chopped finely

1 Half-fill a medium frying pan with water, add chicken; bring to the boil. Reduce heat; simmer, covered, about 5 minutes or until chicken is tender. Drain chicken, discard liquid. Chop chicken finely.

2 Meanwhile, place the water, stock, half the coconut milk, and the ginger, lemon grass, lime leaves, chilli, coriander and sauce in a medium saucepan; bring to the boil. Reduce heat; simmer 15 minutes.

3 Strain liquid; discard solids. Return liquid to the same pan with remaining coconut milk, and the sugar, juice, chicken and mushrooms. Reheat, without boiling. Season to taste.

4 Divide soup into small bowls; sprinkle with extra lime leaves and chillies.

test kitchen tips

For a milder-flavoured soup, remove the seeds and membranes from the chilli as these hold most of the heat.

nutritional count per serving
▶ 8.3g total fat
▶ 6.5g saturated fat
▶ 443kJ (106 cal)
▶ 1.9g carbohydrate
▶ 5.8g protein
▶ 0.8g fibre

sweet soy fried noodles

PREP + COOK TIME 35 MINUTES SERVES 4

440g (14 ounces) fresh wide rice noodles

1 tablespoon peanut oil

3 cloves garlic, sliced thinly

2 eggs, beaten lightly

280g (9 ounces) gai lan, chopped coarsely

200g (6½ ounces) snake beans, cut into 5cm (2-inch) lengths

⅓ cup (80ml) kecap manis

2 tablespoons light soy sauce

½ teaspoon dried chilli flakes

350g (11 ounces) fried tofu, cut into 2cm (¾-inch) cubes

4 green onions (scallions), sliced thinly

¾ cup loosely packed fresh thai basil leaves

1 Place noodles in a large heatproof bowl, cover with boiling water; separate with a fork, drain.
2 Heat oil in a wok over high heat; stir-fry garlic until fragrant. Add egg; stir-fry until set. Add vegetables, sauces and chilli; stir-fry until vegetables are tender. Add noodles, tofu, onion and basil; stir-fry until hot.

tip You can use thick dried rice noodles in this recipe: before using, soak them in boiling water until tender, then drain.

nutritional count per serving
▶ 18.2g total fat   ▶ 55.4g carbohydrate
▶ 4g saturated fat   ▶ 20.1g protein
▶ 2036kJ (487 cal)   ▶ 9.8g fibre

mongolian garlic lamb

PREP + COOK TIME 30 MINUTES **SERVES** 4

3 cloves garlic, crushed

1 tablespoon cornflour (cornstarch)

¼ cup (60ml) dark soy sauce

⅓ cup (80ml) sweet sherry

750g (1½ pounds) lamb backstraps, sliced thinly

2 tablespoons peanut oil

1 tablespoon brown sugar

1 teaspoon sesame oil

8 green onions (scallions), sliced thinly

1 Combine garlic, cornflour, half the sauce and
half the sherry in a large bowl; add lamb, mix well.
2 Heat peanut oil in a wok over high heat; stir-fry
lamb mixture, in batches, until browned.
3 Return lamb to wok with sugar, sesame oil and
remaining sauce and sherry; stir-fry until sauce
thickens slightly. Remove from heat; serve stir-fry
sprinkled with onion.

serving suggestion Steamed rice.

tip The lamb will be easier to cut if you freeze
it for about 20 minutes before slicing.

nutritional count per serving
▶ 28g total fat   ▶ 12.4g carbohydrate
▶ 9.8g saturated fat ▶ 43.1g protein
▶ 2057kJ (492 cal)   ▶ 0.8g fibre

nutritional count per serving
▶ 20.7g total fat
▶ 4.5g saturated fat
▶ 1509kJ (361 cal)
▶ 17.6g carbohydrate
▶ 25.6g protein
▶ 1.9g fibre

test kitchen tips

You can use minced
(ground) chicken in this
recipe instead of the pork.
For information on making
the omelette, see page 113.

mee krob

PREP + COOK TIME 55 MINUTES (+ STANDING) **SERVES** 4

150g (5 ounces) fresh firm silken tofu

vegetable oil, for deep-frying

125g (4 ounces) rice vermicelli noodles

2 tablespoons peanut oil

2 eggs, beaten lightly

1 tablespoon water

2 cloves garlic, crushed

2 fresh small red thai (serrano) chillies, chopped finely

1 fresh small green thai chilli, chopped finely

2 tablespoons grated palm sugar

2 tablespoons fish sauce

2 tablespoons tomato sauce

1 tablespoon rice wine vinegar

200g (6½ ounces) minced (ground) pork

200g (6½ ounces) cooked small prawns (shrimp), shelled, chopped coarsely

6 green onions (scallions), sliced thinly

¼ cup firmly packed fresh coriander (cilantro) leaves

1 Pat tofu all over with absorbent paper; cut into slices, then cut each slice into 1cm (½-inch) wide matchsticks. Spread tofu, in a single layer, on an absorbent-paper-lined tray; cover with more absorbent paper, stand at least 20 minutes.

2 Meanwhile, heat vegetable oil in a wok; deep-fry noodles quickly, in batches, until puffed. Drain on absorbent paper.

3 Using the same heated oil, deep-fry drained tofu, in batches, until browned lightly. Drain on absorbent paper. Discard oil from wok.

4 Heat 2 teaspoons of the peanut oil in cleaned wok over high heat. Pour half of the combined egg and water into wok; cook over medium heat, tilting wok, until almost set. Remove omelette from wok; roll tightly, slice thinly. Heat 2 more teaspoons of the peanut oil in wok; repeat with remaining egg mixture.

5 Combine garlic, chillies, sugar, sauces and vinegar in a small bowl; pour half of the chilli mixture into a small jug, reserve.

6 Combine pork in a bowl with the remaining half of the chilli mixture. Heat remaining peanut oil in wok; stir-fry pork mixture about 5 minutes or until pork is cooked through. Add prawns; stir-fry for 1 minute. Add tofu; stir-fry, tossing gently to combine.

7 Remove wok from heat; add reserved chilli mixture and half of the onion, toss to combine. Add noodles; toss to combine. Sprinkle with remaining onion, omelette strips and coriander.

Always use clean oil for deep-frying; keep it at a constant temperature during cooking. The optimum temperature for vegetables is about 170°C/335°F, and is slightly higher for seafood. Japanese seven-spice mix has a hot kick; its ingredients vary according to region. It is available from Asian supermarkets.

tempura udon

PREP + COOK TIME 30 MINUTES **SERVES** 4

320g (10 ounces) dried thick udon noodles

1 litre (4 cups) dashi

½ cup (125ml) japanese soy sauce

½ cup (125ml) mirin

8 uncooked large king prawns (shrimp) (560g)

vegetable oil, for deep-frying

plain (all-purpose) flour, for dusting

¼ teaspoon japanese seven-spice mix

2 green onions (scallions), chopped finely

TEMPURA BATTER

½ cup (75g) plain (all-purpose) flour

½ cup (75g) cornflour (cornstarch)

1 teaspoon baking powder

1 cup (250ml) iced soda water

1 Cook noodles in a large saucepan of boiling water until tender; drain.
2 Bring dashi, sauce and mirin to the boil in a medium saucepan. Reduce heat; simmer 10 minutes.
3 Meanwhile, shell and devein prawns, leaving tails intact. Score underside of prawns to prevent curling during cooking.
4 Make tempura batter.
5 Heat oil in a small saucepan. Dip prawns, one at a time, in flour, shake off excess; dip in tempura batter. Deep-fry until golden; drain on absorbent paper. Repeat until all prawns are cooked.
6 Just before serving, divide noodles among serving bowls; top with prawns, ladle over broth. Sprinkle with seven-spice mix and onion.

TEMPURA BATTER Combine ingredients in a medium bowl. Do not over-mix; mixture should be lumpy.

nutritional count per serving
▶ 11.5g total fat
▶ 1.7g saturated fat
▶ 2521kJ (603 cal)
▶ 87g carbohydrate
▶ 30g protein
▶ 3.5g fibre

Teppanyaki is traditionally cooked on a grill plate that is on or near the table, and is eaten in batches; a portable electric grill is ideal for this. You could use beef rump or sirloin steak instead of the beef eye fillet used here.

teppanyaki

PREP + COOK TIME 40 MINUTES (+ STANDING) SERVES 4

4 uncooked large king prawns (shrimp) (280g)

500g (1 pound) beef eye fillet, sliced thinly

350g (11¾ ounces) chicken breast fillet, skin on, chopped coarsely

¼ cup (60ml) japanese soy sauce

2 cloves garlic, crushed

1 fresh small red thai (serrano) chilli, chopped finely

4 fresh shiitake mushrooms

1 medium onion (150g), sliced thinly

1 medium red capsicum (bell pepper) (200g), chopped coarsely

4 green onions (scallions), chopped finely

DIPPING SAUCE

½ cup (125ml) japanese soy sauce

1 tablespoon mirin

1 tablespoon brown sugar

2cm (¾-inch) piece fresh ginger (10g), grated

½ teaspoon sesame oil

1 Shell and devein prawns, leaving tails intact. Combine prawns with beef, chicken, sauce, garlic and chilli in a large bowl; stand 15 minutes.

2 Meanwhile, make dipping sauce.

3 Discard mushroom stems; cut a cross in the top of caps.

4 Cook ingredients, except green onion, in batches, on a heated oiled grill plate (or grill or barbecue) until vegetables are just tender, prawns and beef are cooked as you like, and chicken is cooked through.

5 Serve with green onion and dipping sauce.

DIPPING SAUCE Stir ingredients in a medium saucepan until sugar dissolves.

nutritional count per serving
▶ 11.8g total fat
▶ 4.2g saturated fat
▶ 1580kJ (378 cal)
▶ 8.8g carbohydrate
▶ 56.5g protein
▶ 1.7g fibre

AMERICA

cheeseburger with caramelised onion

PREP + COOK TIME **55 MINUTES** SERVES **4**

500g (1 pound) minced (ground) beef

4 thin slices (40g) cheddar

4 hamburger buns, split

1 small tomato (90g), sliced thinly

8 large butter lettuce leaves

4 large dill pickles (240g), sliced thinly

1 tablespoon american-style mustard

⅓ cup (95g) tomato sauce (ketchup)

CARAMELISED ONION

2 tablespoons olive oil

2 medium white onions (300g), sliced thinly

1 tablespoon brown sugar

2 tablespoons balsamic vinegar

2 tablespoons water

1 Make caramelised onion.

2 Shape beef into 4 patties; cook on a heated oiled grill plate (or grill or grill pan) until cooked through. Top each patty with a cheese slice during the last minute of cooking time.

3 Meanwhile, toast buns, cut-sides down, on grill plate.

4 Place cheeseburgers, onion, tomato, lettuce and pickle between buns; serve with mustard and sauce.

CARAMELISED ONION Heat oil in a large frying pan over high heat; cook onion, stirring, about 10 minutes or until soft. Add sugar, vinegar and the water; cook, stirring, about 10 minutes or until onion is caramelised.

serving suggestion French fries or potato wedges.

fish chowder

PREP + COOK TIME 45 MINUTES SERVES 4

45g (1½ ounces) butter

1 large brown onion (200g), chopped coarsely

1 clove garlic, crushed

2 rindless bacon slices (130g), chopped coarsely

2 tablespoons plain (all-purpose) flour

2 medium potatoes (400g), chopped coarsely

3 cups (750ml) milk

2 cups (500ml) vegetable stock

400g (13 ounces) firm white fish fillets, chopped coarsely

2 tablespoons finely chopped fresh chives

1 Melt butter in a large saucepan; cook onion, garlic and bacon, stirring, until onion softens.

2 Add flour to pan; cook, stirring, 1 minute. Add potato, milk and stock; bring to the boil. Reduce heat; simmer, covered, about 10 minutes or until potato is tender.

3 Add fish; simmer, uncovered, about 4 minutes or until fish is barely cooked. Season to taste. Sprinkle soup with chives. Accompany with crusty bread, if you like.

---

nutritional count per serving

▶ 19.5g total fat ▶ 28.4g carbohydrate

▶ 11.6g saturated fat ▶ 34.8g protein

▶ 1810kJ (433 cal) ▶ 2.4g fibre

meatloaf

PREP + COOK TIME 1½ HOURS SERVES 4

750g (1½ pounds) minced (ground) beef

1 cup (70g) stale breadcrumbs

1 medium brown onion (150g), chopped finely

1 egg

2 tablespoons tomato sauce (ketchup)

1 tablespoon worcestershire sauce

185g (6 ounces) canned evaporated milk

2 teaspoons mustard powder

1 tablespoon brown sugar

½ teaspoon mustard powder, extra

¼ cup (60ml) tomato sauce (ketchup), extra

1 Preheat oven to 180°C/350°F. Oil 14cm x 21cm (5-inch x 8½-inch) loaf pan.

2 Combine beef, breadcrumbs, onion, egg, sauces, milk and mustard in a medium bowl. Press mixture into pan. Turn pan upside-down onto a foil-lined oven tray. Leave pan in place. Cook 15 minutes.

3 Meanwhile, combine sugar, extra mustard and extra tomato sauce in a small bowl.

4 Remove meatloaf from oven; remove pan. Brush meatloaf well with sauce mixture, return loaf to oven; cook, uncovered, 45 minutes or until meatloaf is well browned and cooked through. Serve meatloaf with rocket (arugula) leaves and cherry truss tomatoes, if you like.

nutritional count per serving
▶ 19.9g total fat   ▶ 29.1g carbohydrate
▶ 10g saturated fat   ▶ 45.8g protein
▶ 1986kJ (475 cal)   ▶ 1.8g fibre

nutritional count per serving
▶ 69.7g total fat
▶ 22.6g saturated fat
▶ 4585kJ (1097 cal)
▶ 64.3g carbohydrate
▶ 50.4g protein
▶ 6.6g fibre

southern fried chicken with buttermilk mash and gravy

PREP + COOK TIME **55 MINUTES (+ REFRIGERATION)** SERVES **4**

20 chicken drumettes (1.4kg)

1 cup (250ml) buttermilk

1 cup (150g) plain (all-purpose) flour

¼ cup cajun seasoning

½ cup (125ml) vegetable oil

45g (1½ ounces) butter

5 medium potatoes (1kg), chopped coarsely

¾ cup (180ml) buttermilk, extra, warmed

45g (1½ ounces) butter, extra

250g (8 ounces) green beans, trimmed, cut into 4cm (1½-inch) lengths

2 cups (500ml) chicken stock

1 Combine chicken and buttermilk in a large bowl. Cover; refrigerate 3 hours or overnight. Drain; discard buttermilk.

2 Combine flour and seasoning in a large bowl; add chicken pieces, toss to coat in mixture. Cover; refrigerate about 30 minutes or until flour forms a paste.

3 Preheat oven to 240°C/475°F.

4 Heat oil and butter in a large deep frying pan. Shake excess paste from chicken back into the bowl; reserve. Cook chicken, in batches, over medium heat, until browned and crisp.

5 Place chicken on a wire rack over a large baking dish; cook, covered, in oven 15 minutes. Uncover; cook a further 10 minutes or until chicken pieces are cooked through and crisp.

6 Meanwhile, boil, steam or microwave potato until tender; drain. Mash potato in a large bowl with extra buttermilk and butter until smooth. Cover to keep warm.

7 Boil, steam or microwave beans until tender; drain.

8 To make gravy, add reserved paste to pan; cook, stirring, until mixture bubbles. Gradually stir in stock; cook, stirring, until gravy boils and thickens. Strain gravy into a large heatproof jug.

9 Serve chicken with mash, beans and gravy.

pumpkin pie

PREP + COOK TIME **1¾ HOURS (+ REFRIGERATION & COOLING)** SERVES **6**

1 cup (150g) plain (all-purpose) flour

¼ cup (35g) self-raising flour

2 tablespoons cornflour (cornstarch)

2 tablespoons icing (confectioners') sugar

125g (4 ounces) cold butter, chopped

2 tablespoons cold water, approximately

PUMPKIN FILLING

2 eggs

¼ cup (50g) brown sugar

2 tablespoons maple syrup

1 cup cooked mashed pumpkin

⅔ cup (160ml) evaporated milk

1 teaspoon ground cinnamon

½ teaspoon ground nutmeg

pinch ground allspice

1 Sift flours, cornflour and sugar into a medium bowl, rub in butter. Add enough water to make ingredients cling together. Press dough into a ball, knead gently on a floured surface until smooth; cover, refrigerate 30 minutes.

2 Preheat oven to 200°C/400°F.

3 Roll dough on a floured surface until large enough to line a 23cm (9¼-inch) pie plate (or fluted flan pan). Lift pastry into pie plate, ease into side; trim edge. Use scraps of pastry to make a double edge of pastry; trim and decorate edge.

4 Place pie plate on oven tray, line pastry with baking paper, fill with dried beans or rice (see '*blind baking*', page 113). Bake pastry case 10 minutes. Remove paper and beans; bake a further 10 minutes or until browned lightly. Cool pastry case. Reduce oven temperature to 180°C/350°F.

5 Meanwhile, make pumpkin filling.

6 Pour filling into pastry case; bake about 50 minutes or until filling is set, cool. Serve dusted with sifted icing sugar.

PUMPKIN FILLING Beat eggs, sugar and maple syrup in a small bowl with an electric mixer until thick. Stir in pumpkin, milk and spices until combined.

tip You need about 400g (12½ ounces) peeled pumpkin.

Pumpkin pie is the traditional dessert served on Thanksgiving Day in America. European settlers were first introduced to the pumpkin by Native American Indians. The settlers soon realised that pumpkin worked well in both sweet and savoury dishes, and started using it in their pie recipes, substituting it for the spiced fruits they usually used.

nutritional count per serving
▶ 20.1g total fat
▶ 13g saturated fat
▶ 1714kJ (410 cal)
▶ 47.9g carbohydrate
▶ 8.6g protein
▶ 1.7g fibre

SPAIN AND MEXICO

gazpacho

PREP TIME 25 MINUTES (+ REFRIGERATION) SERVES 4

3 cups (750ml) tomato juice

8 medium egg (roma) tomatoes (600g), chopped coarsely

1 medium red onion (170g), chopped coarsely

1 clove garlic

1 lebanese cucumber (130g), chopped coarsely

1 small green capsicum (bell pepper) (150g), chopped coarsely

2 slices white bread, crusts removed, chopped coarsely

2 teaspoons Tabasco sauce

CUCUMBER SALSA

1 small white onion (80g), chopped finely

½ lebanese cucumber (65g), seeded, chopped finely

½ small yellow capsicum (bell pepper) (75g), chopped finely

2 teaspoons olive oil

1 tablespoon vodka

2 tablespoons finely chopped fresh coriander (cilantro)

1 Blend or process juice, tomato, onion, garlic, cucumber, capsicum, bread and sauce, in batches, until smooth. Strain through a sieve into a large bowl. Cover; refrigerate 3 hours.

2 Make cucumber salsa.

3 Serve soup topped with salsa. Serve with crusty bread, if you like.

CUCUMBER SALSA Combine ingredients in a small bowl.

nutritional count per serving
▶ 2.6g total fat
▶ 0.3g saturated fat
▶ 548kJ (131 cal)
▶ 16.9g carbohydrate
▶ 4.8g protein
▶ 4.9g fibre

The traditional paella pan is shallow and wide. If you don't have one, use one large or two smaller frying pans – the mixture should only be about 4cm (1½ inches) deep. This recipe is best made just before serving.

paella valenciana

PREP + COOK TIME 1 HOUR (+ STANDING) SERVES 4

500g (1 pound) clams

1 tablespoon coarse cooking salt (kosher salt)

300g (9½ ounces) uncooked medium king prawns (shrimp)

500g (1 pound) small black mussels

1 pinch saffron threads

¼ cup (60ml) hot water

2 tablespoons olive oil

2 chicken thigh fillets (400g), chopped coarsely

1 cured chorizo sausage (170g), sliced thinly

1 large red onion (300g), chopped finely

1 medium red capsicum (bell pepper) (200g), chopped finely

2 cloves garlic, crushed

2 teaspoons sweet paprika

1½ cups (300g) white medium-grain rice

3½ cups (875ml) chicken stock

1 cup (120g) frozen peas

2 medium tomatoes (300g), peeled, seeded, chopped finely

1 Rinse clams under cold water; place in a large bowl, sprinkle with salt, cover with cold water, stand 2 hours. Discard water; rinse clams thoroughly, drain.

2 Shell and devein prawns, leaving tails intact. Scrub mussels, remove beards.

3 Combine saffron and the hot water in a small bowl; stand 30 minutes.

4 Heat oil in a 40cm (16-inch) wide shallow pan; cook chicken until browned. Remove from pan.

5 Cook chorizo in same pan until browned; drain on absorbent paper. Add onion, capsicum, garlic and paprika; cook, stirring, until soft. Add rice; stir to coat in onion mixture. Return chicken and chorizo to pan.

6 Stir in stock and saffron mixture; bring to the boil. Reduce heat; simmer, uncovered, about 12 minutes or until rice is almost tender. Sprinkle peas and tomato over rice; simmer, uncovered, 3 minutes.

7 Place clams, mussels and prawns over rice mixture (do not stir to combine); cover pan. Simmer about 5 minutes or until prawns change colour and clams and mussels have opened. Season to taste.

nutritional count per serving

▶ 31.4g total fat
▶ 8.9g saturated fat
▶ 3319kJ (794 cal)
▶ 72.4g carbohydrate
▶ 53.2g protein
▶ 4.7g fibre

nutritional count per piece

▶ 3.2g total fat
▶ 1.3g saturated fat
▶ 238kJ (57 cal)
▶ 4.3g carbohydrate
▶ 2.4g protein
▶ 0.6g fibre

Pronounced 'cheh-pote-lay', chipotle is the name used for jalapeño chillies once they've been dried and smoked. Chipotles have a deep, intensely smoky flavour, rather than a searing heat, and are dark brown, almost black in colour and wrinkled in appearance. You can also find them in cans from Spanish delicatessens. If using canned chipotles, add them to the processor in step 3.

chipotle beef tostaditas

PREP + COOK TIME 55 MINUTES (+ STANDING) **MAKES** 36

2 chipotle chillies

½ cup (125ml) boiling water

12 x 17cm (6¾-inch) round white corn tortillas

vegetable oil, for deep-frying

1 tablespoon vegetable oil, extra

1 small brown onion (80g), sliced thinly

1 clove garlic, crushed

280g (9 ounces) minced (ground) beef

1 tablespoon tomato paste

1 cup (250ml) beer

¼ cup coarsely chopped fresh coriander (cilantro)

½ cup (120g) sour cream

1 Cover chillies with the boiling water in a small heatproof bowl; stand 20 minutes.

2 Meanwhile, using a 7cm (2¾-inch) round cutter, cut 3 rounds from each tortilla. Heat oil in a wok; deep-fry rounds, in batches, until browned lightly. Drain tortilla crisps on absorbent paper. (Remove oil; reserve for use in other recipes.)

3 Drain chillies over a small bowl; reserve liquid. Discard stems from chillies. Blend or process chillies and reserved liquid until smooth.

4 Heat extra vegetable oil in a medium frying pan over high heat; cook onion, stirring, until softened. Add garlic and beef; cook, stirring, until beef is changed in colour. Stir in paste, beer and chilli puree; bring to the boil. Reduce heat; simmer, uncovered, about 15 minutes or until liquid is almost evaporated. Season to taste. Stir in coriander.

5 Top each tortilla crisp with a rounded teaspoon of chipotle beef and ½ teaspoon of sour cream.

fajitas

PREP + COOK TIME 45 MINUTES SERVES 4

600g (1¼ pounds) lamb strips

3 cloves garlic, crushed

¼ cup (60ml) lemon juice

2 teaspoons ground cumin

1 tablespoon olive oil

1 large red capsicum (bell pepper) (350g), sliced thickly

1 large green capsicum (bell pepper) (350g), sliced thickly

1 medium yellow capsicum (bell pepper) (200g), sliced thickly

1 large red onion (300g), sliced thickly

8 large flour tortillas

GUACAMOLE

1 large avocado (320g), chopped coarsely

¼ cup finely chopped fresh coriander (cilantro)

1 tablespoon lime juice

1 small white onion (80g), chopped finely

SALSA CRUDA

2 medium tomatoes (300g), seeded, chopped finely

1 fresh long red chilli, chopped finely

½ cup coarsely chopped fresh coriander (cilantro)

1 clove garlic, crushed

1 small white onion (80g), chopped finely

2 tablespoons lime juice

1 Combine lamb, garlic, juice, cumin and oil in a large bowl. Cover; refrigerate.

2 Make guacamole. Make salsa cruda.

3 Cook lamb, in batches, in a heated oiled frying pan over high heat, stirring, until browned all over and cooked as desired. Remove from pan. Cover to keep warm.

4 Cook capsicum and onion, in batches, in the same pan, stirring, until just softened.

5 Meanwhile, heat tortillas according to instructions on packet.

6 Return lamb and capsicum mixture to pan; stir gently over medium heat until hot. Season to taste. Divide fajita mixture among serving plates; serve with tortillas, guacamole and salsa cruda.

GUACAMOLE Gently combine ingredients in a small bowl. Season to taste.

SALSA CRUDA Combine ingredients in a small bowl. Season to taste.

nutritional count per serving
▶ 37.5g total fat
▶ 10.4g saturated fat
▶ 3227kJ (772 cal)
▶ 62.3g carbohydrate
▶ 45.8g protein
▶ 8.4g fibre

bean nachos

PREP + COOK TIME 20 MINUTES SERVES 6

2 x 410g (13 ounces) canned kidney beans, rinsed, drained

⅓ cup (85g) chunky tomato salsa

⅓ cup finely chopped fresh coriander (cilantro)

220g (7 ounces) corn chips

1½ cups (180g) coarsely grated cheddar cheese

2 cups (120g) finely shredded iceberg lettuce

1 small tomato (90g), chopped coarsely

½ small avocado (100g), chopped coarsely

2 tablespoons lime juice

1 Preheat oven to 220°C/425°F.

2 Combine half the beans with salsa; mash until chunky. Stir in remaining beans and coriander.

3 Spread half the corn chips in a medium shallow baking dish; top with half the cheese and half the bean mixture. Top with remaining corn chips, remaining cheese, then remaining bean mixture. Bake 10 minutes.

4 Toss lettuce, tomato and avocado in a medium bowl with juice. Serve nachos topped with salad.

nutritional count per serving

▶ 24.5g total fat

▶ 11.6g saturated fat

▶ 1856kJ (444 cal)

▶ 33.7g carbohydrate

▶ 17.3g protein

▶ 10.8g fibre

crème catalana

PREP + COOK TIME 25 MINUTES (+ REFRIGERATION) **SERVES** 8

8 egg yolks

1 cup (220g) caster (superfine) sugar

1.25 litres (5 cups) milk

2 teaspoons finely grated lemon rind

1 cinnamon stick

½ cup (75g) cornflour (cornstarch)

⅓ cup (75g) caster (superfine) sugar, extra

1 Whisk egg yolks and sugar in a large bowl until creamy.

2 Place 1 litre (4 cups) of the milk, rind and cinnamon in a large saucepan; stir over medium heat until mixture just comes to the boil. Remove immediately from heat.

3 Strain milk mixture into a large heatproof jug; pour milk into egg mixture, whisking constantly. Stir remaining milk and the cornflour in a small jug until smooth; add to egg mixture.

4 Return mixture to pan; stir constantly over heat until mixture boils and thickens.

5 Pour mixture into a 26cm (10½-inch) heatproof pie dish. Cover; refrigerate 4 hours or overnight.

6 Just before serving, preheat grill (broiler).

7 Sprinkle custard with extra sugar. Place under grill until sugar is caramelised. Serve immediately.

nutritional count per serving
- 11.2g total fat
- 5.4g saturated fat
- 1392kJ (333 cal)
- 52.3g carbohydrate
- 7.9g protein
- 0g fibre

AUSTRALIA

meat pie

PREP + COOK TIME 1¾ HOURS (+ REFRIGERATION & COOLING) MAKES 6

1½ cups (225g) plain (all-purpose) flour

90g (3 ounces) cold butter, chopped coarsely

1 egg

1 tablespoon iced water, approximately

2 sheets puff pastry

1 egg, extra

BEEF FILLING

1 tablespoon vegetable oil

1 small brown onion (80g), chopped finely

625g (1¼ pounds) minced (ground) beef

410g (13 ounces) canned crushed tomatoes

2 tablespoons tomato paste

2 tablespoons worcestershire sauce

¾ cup (180ml) beef stock

1 Process flour and butter until crumbly. Add egg and enough of the water to make ingredients cling together. Knead pastry on a floured surface until smooth. Cover; refrigerate 30 minutes.

2 Meanwhile, make beef filling.

3 Oil six ⅔-cup (160ml) pie tins. Divide pastry into six equal portions; roll each between sheets of baking paper until large enough to line tins. Lift pastry into tins; gently press over bases and sides; trim. Refrigerate 30 minutes.

4 Cut six 11cm (4½-inch) rounds from puff pastry. Refrigerate until required.

5 Preheat oven to 200°C/400°F.

6 Place pastry cases on an oven tray; line pastry with baking paper then fill with dried beans or rice (see 'blind baking', page 113). Bake pastry cases for 10 minutes; remove paper and beans. Bake a further 5 minutes; cool.

7 Fill pastry cases with cooled beef filling; brush edges of pastry with extra egg. Top with puff pastry rounds; press edges to seal. Brush tops with egg. Cut small steam holes in top of pies. Bake about 20 minutes or until pastry is golden. Serve pies with chips and accompany with tomato sauce (ketchup), if you like.

BEEF FILLING Heat oil in a large saucepan over high heat, add onion and beef; cook, stirring, until beef is well browned. Stir in tomatoes, paste, sauce and stock; bring to the boil. Reduce heat, simmer, uncovered, about 20 minutes or until thick. Season to taste. Cool.

nutritional count per pie
▶ 38.7g total fat
▶ 13.8g saturated fat
▶ 2876kJ (688 cal)
▶ 52.4g carbohydrate
▶ 31.2g protein
▶ 3.5g fibre

tuna mornay

PREP + COOK TIME 10 MINUTES SERVES 4

30g (1 ounce) butter

1 medium brown onion (150g), chopped finely

1 stalk celery (150g), trimmed, chopped finely

1 tablespoon plain (all-purpose) flour

¾ cup (180ml) milk

½ cup (125ml) pouring cream

⅓ cup (40g) grated cheddar

130g (4 ounces) canned corn kernels, drained

2 x 185g (6 ounces) canned tuna, drained

1 cup (70g) stale breadcrumbs

¼ cup (30g) grated cheddar, extra

1 Preheat oven to 180°C/350°F.

2 Melt butter in a medium saucepan over high heat; cook onion and celery, stirring, until onion is soft. Add flour; cook, stirring, 1 minute. Gradually stir in combined milk and cream; cook, stirring, until mixture boils and thickens. Remove pan from heat, add cheese, corn and tuna; stir until cheese is melted. Season to taste.

3 Spoon mornay mixture into four 1½-cup (375ml) ovenproof dishes. Sprinkle mornay with combined breadcrumbs and extra cheese.

4 Bake tuna mornay about 15 minutes or until heated through.

serving suggestion A green leafy salad.

nutritional count per serving
- ▶ 30.2g total fat
- ▶ 18.8g saturated fat
- ▶ 2031kJ (486 cal)
- ▶ 23.4g carbohydrate
- ▶ 29.3g protein
- ▶ 2.5g fibre

damper

PREP + COOK TIME 45 MINUTES SERVES 6

3 cups (450g) self-raising flour

30g (1 ounce) butter

½ cup (125ml) milk

1 cup (250ml) water, approximately

1 Preheat oven to 180°C/350°F. Grease oven tray.
2 Sift flour into a large bowl; rub in butter. Make
a well in the centre, add milk and enough water to
mix into a soft sticky dough. Knead on a floured
surface until smooth.
3 Press dough into a 15cm (6-inch) circle, place
on tray. Cut a cross through dough, about 1cm
(½-inch) deep. Brush top with a little extra milk or
water; dust with a little extra flour.
4 Bake for 30 minutes or until damper sounds
hollow when tapped. Accompany with butter and
golden syrup, or a little jam, if you like.

nutritional count per serving
▶ 5.8g total fat   ▶ 53.9g carbohydrate
▶ 3.4g saturated fat   ▶ 8.1g protein
▶ 1292kJ (309 cal)   ▶ 2.9g fibre

roast lamb dinner

PREP + COOK TIME 1¾ HOURS SERVES 6

2kg (4-pound) leg of lamb

3 sprigs fresh rosemary, chopped coarsely

½ teaspoon sweet paprika

1kg (2 pounds) potatoes, chopped coarsely

500g (1 pound) pumpkin, chopped coarsely

3 small brown onions (240g), halved

2 tablespoons olive oil

2 tablespoons plain (all-purpose) flour

1 cup (250ml) chicken stock

¼ cup (60ml) dry red wine

CAULIFLOWER MORNAY

1 small cauliflower (1kg), cut into florets

45g (1½ ounces) butter

¼ cup (35g) plain (all-purpose) flour

2 cups (500ml) milk

¾ cup (90g) coarsely grated cheddar

1 Preheat oven to 200°C/400°F.

2 Place lamb in an oiled large flameproof baking dish; using a sharp knife, score skin at 2cm (¾-inch) intervals, sprinkle with rosemary and paprika. Roast lamb 15 minutes.

3 Reduce oven temperature to 180°C/350°F. Roast lamb about 45 minutes or until cooked as desired.

4 Meanwhile, place potatoes, pumpkin and onions, in a single layer, in a large shallow baking dish; drizzle with oil. Roast for the last 45 minutes of lamb cooking time.

5 Meanwhile, make cauliflower mornay.

6 Remove lamb and vegetables from oven; strain pan juices from lamb into a medium jug. Cover lamb and vegetables to keep warm. Return ¼ cup of the pan juices to baking dish, stir in flour; stir over medium heat about 5 minutes or until mixture bubbles and browns. Gradually add stock and wine; stir over high heat until gravy boils and thickens. Strain gravy into a medium heatproof jug.

7 Slice lamb; serve with roasted vegetables, cauliflower mornay and gravy.

CAULIFLOWER MORNAY Boil, steam or microwave cauliflower until tender; drain. Melt butter in a medium saucepan over high heat, add flour; cook, stirring, until mixture bubbles and thickens. Gradually add milk; cook, stirring, until mixture boils and thickens. Stir in half the cheese. Preheat grill (broiler). Place cauliflower in a 1.5-litre (6-cup) shallow flameproof dish; pour mornay sauce over cauliflower, sprinkle with remaining cheese. Grill until browned lightly.

nutritional count per serving
- ▶ 35.6g total fat
- ▶ 17g saturated fat
- ▶ 3244kJ (776 cal)
- ▶ 40.5g carbohydrate
- ▶ 71.9g protein
- ▶ 7g fibre

pavlova

PREP + COOK TIME **2 HOURS (+ COOLING)** SERVES **8**

4 egg whites

1 cup (220g) caster (superfine) sugar

½ teaspoon vanilla extract

¾ teaspoon white vinegar

300ml (½ pint) thickened (heavy) cream

250g (8 ounces) strawberries

¼ cup (60ml) passionfruit pulp

1 Preheat oven to 130°C/260°F. Line oven tray with baking paper; mark a 18cm (7¼-inch) circle on paper, turn paper over.

2 Beat egg whites in a small bowl with an electric mixer until soft peaks form; gradually add sugar, beating until sugar dissolves. Add extract and vinegar; beat until combined.

3 Spread meringue inside the circle on the baking paper, building it up to 8cm (3¼-inch) in height. Using a spatula, gently smooth side and top of pavlova; mark decorative grooves around side of pavlova, smooth top again.

4 Bake pavlova about 1½ hours. Turn oven off; cool pavlova in oven with door ajar.

5 Whip cream until soft peaks form. Cut strawberries in half. Cut around top edge of pavlova (the crisp meringue top will fall on top of the marshmallow centre). Top pavlova with cream, strawberries and passionfruit.

nutritional count per serving
- ▶ 14.5g total fat
- ▶ 9.5g saturated fat
- ▶ 1078kJ (258 cal)
- ▶ 30g carbohydrate
- ▶ 3.4g protein
- ▶ 1.7g fibre

COOKING TECHNIQUES

Eggplant parmigiana (1) (page 13) Using a vegetable peeler, peel off random strips of skin from the eggplant. Slice the eggplant thinly using a sharp knife.

Eggplant parmigiana (2) (page 13) Dip the eggplant slices in the flour to coat all over, then shake off excess. Dip the eggplant into beaten egg, then coat with breadcrumbs.

Vegetable pithiviers (page 24) Centre a 9cm-round cutter on pastry. Layer a quarter of the mushroom mixture, zucchini and capsicum on the pastry; remove cutter. The round pastry cutter holds the vegetables in place while layering.

Chicken, spinach and cheese gözleme (page 52) Fold the top section of the pastry over the chicken filling, then fold the bottom section up; tuck in the ends to enclose the filling.

Minestrone (1) (page 6) Roast the ham hock and onion in a preheated 220°C/425°F oven for about 30 minutes or until cooked. The roasted hock and onion adds a rich flavour to the soup.

Minestrone (2) (page 6) Remove the ham from the hock and, using two forks, shred the meat coarsely. Discard the bone, fat and skin. Add meat to the pan to make the tomato-based broth for the minestrone.

Yorkshire puddings (page 42) Spoon oil into eight holes of a muffin pan; heat in a 220°C/425°F oven until quite hot, then remove from oven and pour in the yorkshire pudding batter. Return the pan to the hot oven quickly so the puddings will start to cook right away.

Washing leeks removes any sandy grit from the inside layers. Cut in half lengthwise, stopping at the root. Fan the layers out and wash under fast-running cold water. Flick the leek to remove excess water.

Mee krob (page 81) To make a thin omelette, lightly whisk the eggs, then pour into a heated lightly-oiled wok. Tilt the pan to cover the base of the wok with the egg; cook until the egg is set.

Boeuf bourguignon (1) (page 16) When peeling the baby brown onions, remove the skin but leave the roots intact. It's important that the onions remain whole while the bourguignon slowly cooks.

Boeuf bourguignon (2) (page 16) Cook the coarsely chopped beef in batches in a flameproof dish until they're browned. If you cook too many pieces at a time, they'll stew rather than brown.

Boeuf bourguignon (3) (page 16) Once the beef and onion are browned lightly, sprinkle the flour over the mixture and stir until the mixture bubbles and thickens.

Pitting an olive is easy with on olive pitter, pictured; put the olive in the cup and push, and out pops the seed. To do this by hand, crush the olive with the flat side of a large knife and slip the seed out.

A mortar and pestle is great for crushing, grinding or blending spices. To crush peppercorns, place them in the mortar (bowl) and pound vigorously with the pestle.

Toasting nuts Whether it's almonds, peanuts, pistachios, or any other nut, toasting them is the same. Stir nuts over a low heat in a dry frying pan until golden brown. Remove the nuts immediately from the pan to stop them from burning.

Blind baking is when a pastry case is baked before the filling is added. Cover the pastry with baking paper; fill it with dried beans or uncooked rice. Cook the pastry for 10 minutes, then remove the paper and beans, and cook it for 10 minutes more (or as directed in the recipe), or until the pastry is golden.

GLOSSARY

ALLSPICE also known as pimento or jamaican pepper; tastes like a combination of nutmeg, cumin, clove and cinnamon. Available whole or ground.

ALMONDS
blanched brown skins removed.
flaked paper-thin slices.
ground (meal) nuts are powdered to a coarse flour-like texture.
slivered small pieces cut lengthways.

BACON SLICES bacon rashers.

BAKING POWDER a raising agent consisting mainly of two parts cream of tartar to one part bicarbonate of soda (baking soda).

BASIL an aromatic herb; there are many types, but the most commonly used is sweet, or common, basil.
thai also known as horapa; different from sweet basil in both look and taste, having smaller leaves, purplish stems, and a slight licorice or aniseed taste.

BEANS
snake long (about 40cm/16 inches), thin, round, fresh green beans; Asian in origin, with a taste similar to green or french beans. Used frequently in stir-fries, they are also known as yard-long beans because of their (pre-metric) length.
white in this book, some recipes may simply call for 'white beans', a generic term we use for canned or dried navy, cannellini, haricot or great northern beans, all of which can be substituted for the other.

BEEF
chuck inexpensive cut from the neck and shoulder area; good slow-cooked.
gravy boneless stewing beef from the shin; slow-cooked, imbues stocks, soups and casseroles with a gelatine richness. Cut crossways with the bone, is osso buco.
topside roast (silverside) the actual cut used for making corned beef (usually sold vacuum-sealed in brine).

BICARBONATE OF SODA also called baking soda.

BLACK MUSSELS buy from a reliable fish market: must be tightly closed when bought, indicating they are alive. Before cooking, scrub shells with a strong brush and remove the beards.

BLACK PEPPERCORNS picked when the berry is not quite ripe, then dried until it shrivels and the skin turns dark brown to black. A strongly-flavoured pepper.

BREADCRUMBS
fresh bread is processed into crumbs.
packaged fine-textured, crunchy white breadcrumbs; good for coating foods that are to be fried.
stale crumbs made by blending or processing 1- or 2-day-old bread.

BURGHUL also called bulghur wheat; hulled steamed wheat kernels that, once dried, are crushed into various-sized grains. Is not the same as cracked wheat.

BUTTER we use salted butter unless stated otherwise; 125g (4 ounces) is equal to 1 stick of butter.

BUTTERMILK originally the term given to the slightly sour liquid left after butter was churned from cream, today it is commercially made similarly to yoghurt. Sold alongside all fresh milk products in supermarkets. Despite the implication of its name, it is low in fat.

CALASPARRA RICE a short-grain rice available from gourmet-food stores and Spanish delicatessens. If you can't find calasparra, any short-grain rice can be substituted.

CHEESE
fetta Greek in origin; a crumbly textured cheese made from sheep or goat's milk, it has a sharp, salty taste.
gruyère a Swiss cheese with small holes and a nutty, slightly salty, flavour.
mozzarella a soft, spun-curd cheese originating in Italy; it is a popular pizza cheese because of its low melting point and elasticity when heated.
ricotta a soft, sweet cow's-milk cheese with a low-fat content and a slightly grainy, moist, texture. The name roughly translates as 'cooked again' and refers to its manufacture from a whey that is itself a by-product of other cheese making.

CHICKEN
barbecued we use barbecued chickens weighing about 900g (1¾ pounds). With the skin and bones removed, this size provides 4 cups of shredded meat or about 3 cups of coarsely chopped meat.
breast fillet breast halved, skinned and boned.
drumette small fleshy part of the wing between shoulder and elbow, trimmed to resemble a drumstick.
tenderloin thin strip of meat lying just under the breast; good for stir-frying.
thigh fillet thigh with skin and centre bone removed.

CHICKPEAS also called garbanzo beans, hummus or channa; an irregularly round, sandy-coloured legume.

CHILLI
fresh long available both fresh and dried; a generic term used for any moderately hot, long, thin chilli.
red thai (serrano) small, very hot and bright red in colour.
chipotle smoked jalapeño chillies. Available dried or canned from specialty food retailers and delicatessens.

COCONUT MILK not the liquid found inside the fruit (coconut water), but the diluted liquid from the second pressing of the white flesh of a mature coconut (the first pressing produces coconut cream). Available in cans and cartons at most supermarkets.

CORIANDER also called cilantro, pak chee or chinese parsley; bright-green-leafed herb with both a pungent aroma and taste. Used as an ingredient in a wide variety of cuisines. Often stirred into or sprinkled over a dish just before serving for maximum impact as, like other leafy herbs, its characteristics diminish with cooking. Both the stems and roots of coriander are used in Thai cooking: wash well before chopping. Coriander seeds are dried and sold either whole or ground, and neither form tastes remotely like the fresh leaf.

CORNFLOUR (cornstarch) available made from corn or wheat; used as a thickening agent in cooking.

COUSCOUS a grain-like cereal product made from semolina. A semolina flour and water dough is sieved then dehydrated to produce minuscule even-sized pellets; it is rehydrated by steaming or adding a warm liquid, and swells to three or four times its original size; eaten as a side dish or salad ingredient.

CREAM
pouring also called pure or single cream. It has no additives and contains a minimum fat content of 35%.
sour a thick, commercially-cultured sour cream with a minimum fat content of 35%.
thickened a whipping cream containing a thickener. Minimum fat content 35%.

CURRY POWDER/PASTES a blend of ground spices used for making Indian and some South-Asian dishes. Available as mild or hot.

CUSTARD POWDER instant mixture used to make pouring custard; similar to North American instant pudding mixes.

DASHI the basic fish and seaweed stock that accounts for the distinctive flavour of many Japanese dishes, such as soups and various casserole dishes. Made from dried bonito (a type of tuna) flakes and kombu (kelp); instant dashi is available in granules, liquid concentrate and powder from Asian food shops.

EGGS we use large chicken eggs weighing an average of 60g (2 ounces) unless stated otherwise. If a recipe calls for raw or barely cooked eggs, exercise caution if there is a salmonella problem in your area, particularly in food eaten by children and pregnant women.

EVAPORATED MILK has had about 60 per cent of the water removed via evaporation; it differs from condensed milk in that it has no added sugar, whereas condensed milk, which also has about 60 per cent of the water removed, has sugar added. Adding the correct proportion of water to evaporated milk will constitute it to a rough equivalent of fresh milk.

FISH FILLETS, FIRM WHITE white fish means non-oily fish; includes bream, flathead, whiting, snapper, dhufish, redfish and ling. Check for any small pieces of bone in the fillets and use tweezers to remove them.

FLAT-LEAF PARSLEY also known as continental parsley or italian parsley.

FLOUR
plain (all-purpose) made from wheat.
self-raising (self-rising) all-purpose plain or wholemeal flour with baking powder added; make it yourself in the proportion of 1 cup flour to 2 teaspoons baking powder.

FRIED SHALLOTS are served as a condiment at Asian mealtimes, or sprinkled over just-cooked food to provide an extra crunchy finish to a salad, stir-fry or curry. They can be purchased at all Asian grocery stores; once opened, they will keep for months if stored in a tightly sealed glass jar. Make your own by frying thinly sliced peeled shallots or baby onions until golden brown and crisp.

GLACÉ FRUIT SALAD fruit, such as peaches, pears, pineapple, apricot and orange, cooked in a heavy sugar syrup.

GREEN GINGER WINE a beverage that is 14% alcohol by volume, with the taste of fresh ginger. You can substitute it with dry (white) vermouth, if you prefer.

JAPANESE SEVEN-SPICE MIX (shichimi-togarashi, seven-spice blend) a commonly used Japanese spice blend that typically includes roasted citrus peel, sesame seeds, hot chillies, japanese pepper and ginger. It is used to flavour food, or as a condiment sprinkled over food.

JELLY CRYSTALS a powdered mixture of gelatine, sweetener and artificial fruit flavouring used to make a moulded, translucent, quivering dessert. Also known as jello.

KAFFIR LIME LEAVES also called bai magrood. A strip of fresh lime peel may be substituted for each kaffir lime leaf.

KECAP MANIS, see sauce, soy.

LAMB
backstrap also known as eye of loin; the larger fillet from a row of loin chops or cutlets. Tender, and are best cooked rapidly on the barbecue or pan-fried.
leg cut from the hindquarter; can be boned, butterflied, rolled and tied, or diced into pieces.
shoulder a large piece having much connective tissue so is best pot-roasted or braised.

LEBANESE CUCUMBERS a short, slender and thin-skinned cucumber. Probably the most popular variety because of its tender, edible skin, tiny, yielding seeds, and sweet, fresh and flavoursome taste.

LENTILS (RED, BROWN, YELLOW) dried pulses often identified by and named after their colour.
french green are a local cousin to the famous (and very expensive) French lentils du puy; green-blue, tiny lentils with a nutty, earthy flavour and a hardy nature that allows them to be rapidly cooked without disintegrating.

MAPLE SYRUP distilled from the sap of sugar maple trees. Most often eaten with pancakes or waffles, but also used as an ingredient in baking or in desserts. Maple-flavoured syrup or pancake syrup are not adequate substitutes.

MINT the most commonly used variety of mint is spearmint; it has pointed, bright-green leaves and a fresh flavour.

MIRIN a Japanese champagne-coloured cooking wine, made of glutinous rice and alcohol. It is used just for cooking and should not be confused with sake.

MUSTARD
american-style a sweet mustard containing mustard seeds, sugar, salt, spices and garlic; is bright yellow in colour. Served with hamburgers and hot dogs.
powder finely ground white (yellow) mustard seeds.
seeds, black also known as brown mustard seeds; more pungent than the white variety. Used frequently in curries.
wholegrain also known as seeded mustard. A french-style coarse-grain mustard made from crushed mustard seeds and dijon-style french mustard.

NUTMEG a strong and pungent spice ground from the dried nut of an Indonesian evergreen tree. Usually found ground, though the flavour is more intense from a whole nut, which is available from spice shops, so it's best to grate your own. Also found in mixed spice mixtures.

NUTS, TOASTING toasting brings out the flavour of nuts: Place nuts in a single layer in a dry frying pan and cook over a low heat until fragrant and just changed in colour; remove from pan immediately. They may also be roasted in a single layer in a pan in a moderately slow oven (160°C/325°F) for 8 to 10 minutes. Be careful to avoid burning nuts.

OREGANO a herb, also known as wild marjoram; has a woody stalk and clumps of tiny, dark-green leaves. Has a pungent, peppery flavour.

PASSATA sieved tomato puree. To substitute, puree and sieve canned tomatoes, or use canned tomato puree, which is similar, but slightly thicker. Available from supermarkets.

PASTRY
fillo is unique in that no fat or margarine is added to the dough. The dough is very elastic in texture and not rolled like other pastries, but stretched to the desired thickness. This gives it its delicate, tissue-thin sheets. Brush with butter or margarine before baking.
puff a crisp, light pastry; layers of dough and margarine are folded and rolled many times making many layers. When baked, it becomes a high, crisp, flaky pastry.

RAS EL HANOUT the name means 'top of the shop' and the mixture varies from one merchant to another, but is always subtly savoury with a touch of heat.

SAGE a pungent herb with narrow, grey-green leaves; slightly bitter with a slightly musty mint aroma. Refrigerate fresh sage wrapped in absorbent paper and sealed in a plastic bag for up to four days. Dried sage comes whole, crumbled or ground. Store in a cool, dark place for no more than three months.

SAUCE

soy also called sieu; made from fermented soya beans. Several variations are available in supermarkets and Asian food stores; we use japanese soy sauce unless indicated otherwise.

dark soy is deep brown, almost black in colour; rich, with a thicker consistency than other types. Pungent but not particularly salty; good for marinating.

japanese soy an all-purpose low-sodium soy sauce with more wheat content than its Chinese counterparts; fermented in barrels and aged. Possibly the best table soy and the one to choose if you only want one variety.

kecap manis a dark, thick sweet soy sauce used in most South-East Asian cuisines. Depending on the manufacturer, the sauces's sweetness is derived from the addition of either molasses or palm sugar when brewed.

light soy fairly thin in consistency and, while paler than the others, the saltiest tasting; used in dishes in which the natural colour of the ingredients is to be maintained. Not to be confused with salt-reduced or low-sodium soy sauces.

fish called naam pla if from Thailand, or nuoc naam if fromVietnam, though the two are almost identical. Made from pulverised salted fermented fish (most often anchovies); has a pungent smell and strong taste. Available in varying degrees of intensity, so use according to your taste.

sweet chilli a fairly mild sauce made from chillies, sugar, garlic and vinegar.

tomato also known as ketchup or catsup; a flavoured condiment made from tomatoes, vinegar and spices.

worcestershire a dark coloured condiment made from garlic, soy sauce, tamarind, onions, molasses, anchovies, lime, vinegar and other seasonings. Available in most supermarkets.

STERILISING JARS it's important the jars be as clean as possible; make sure your hands, the preparation area, tea towels and cloths etc, are clean, too. The aim is to finish sterilising the jars and lids at the same time the preserve is ready to be bottled; the hot preserve should be bottled into hot, dry clean jars. Jars that aren't sterilised properly can cause deterioration of the preserves during storage. Always start with cleaned washed jars and lids, then follow one of these methods:
(1) Put the jars and lids through the hottest cycle of a dishwasher without using any detergent, or
(2) Lie the jars down in a boiler with the lids, cover them with cold water then cover the boiler with a lid. Bring the water to the boil over a high heat and boil the jars for 20 minutes, or
(3) Stand the jars upright, without touching each other, on a wooden board on the lowest shelf in the oven. Turn the oven to the lowest possible temperature, close the oven door and leave the jars to heat through for 30 minutes.
Next, remove the jars from the oven or dishwasher with a towel, or from the boiling water with tongs and rubber-gloved hands; the water will evaporate from hot wet jars quite quickly.
Stand the jars upright and not touching each other on a wooden board, or a bench covered with a clean towel, to protect and insulate the bench. Fill the jars as directed in the recipe; secure the lids tightly, holding jars firmly with a towel or an oven mitt. Leave preserves at room temperature to cool before storing.

SULTANAS dried grapes, also known as golden raisins.

TAMARIND CONCENTRATE (or paste) a popular souring agent in Southern India. The commercial result of the distillation of tamarind juice into a condensed, compacted paste. Thick and purple-black, it is ready-to-use, with no soaking or straining required; can be diluted with water according to taste. Gives a sweet-sour, slightly astringent taste to food. Substitute with lemon or lime juice.

TOFU (bean curd) an off-white, custard-like product made from the 'milk' of crushed soya beans. Refrigerate fresh tofu in water (changed daily) for up to four days.

fried pieces of bean curd that have been deep-fried until the surface is brown and crusty and the inside almost dry.

silken refers to the method by which it is made – strained through silk.

TOMATO

canned whole peeled tomatoes in natural juices; available crushed, chopped or diced. Use undrained.

egg also called roma or plum, these are smallish, oval-shaped tomatoes often used in Italian cooking.

paste triple-concentrated tomato puree.

semi-dried partially dried tomato pieces in olive oil; softer and juicier than sun-dried. These are not a preserve so do not keep as long as sun-dried.

sun-dried dehydrated tomato pieces. We use sun-dried tomatoes packaged in oil, unless otherwise specified.

TORTILLAS thin, round unleavened bread originating in Mexico. Two kinds are available, one made from wheat flour and the other from corn (maize meal).

VEAL SCHNITZEL thinly sliced steak available crumbed or plain; we used plain schnitzel in our recipes.

VINEGAR

balsamic originally from Modena, Italy, there are now many balsamic vinegars on the market ranging in pungency and quality depending on how, and for how long, they have been aged. Quality can be determined up to a point by price; use the most expensive sparingly.

cider made from fermented apples.

red wine based on fermented red wine.

rice a colourless vinegar made from fermented rice and flavoured with sugar and salt. Also called seasoned rice vinegar; sherry can be substituted.

white made from spirit of cane sugar.

white wine made from white wine.

rice wine made from rice wine lees (sediment), salt and alcohol.

YEAST raising agent used in dough making. Granular (7g sachets) and fresh compressed (20g blocks) yeast can almost always be substituted one for the other when yeast is called for.

YOGHURT we use plain full-cream yoghurt unless noted otherwise.

greek-style a full-cream yoghurt, often made from sheep milk; its thick, smooth consistency, almost like whipped cream, is attained by draining off milk liquids. A good yoghurt to use in cooking.

INDEX

Published in 2013 by Bauer Media Books, Sydney
Bauer Media Books is a division of Bauer Media Limited.

MEDIA GROUP

BAUER MEDIA BOOKS
Publishing director Gerry Reynolds
Publisher Sally Wright
Director of sales, marketing & rights Brian Cearnes
Editorial & food director Pamela Clark
Creative director & designer Hieu Chi Nguyen
Senior editor Wendy Bryant
Food concept director Sophia Young
Food editor Emma Braz
Special sales manager Simone Aquilina
Marketing manager Bridget Cody
Senior business analyst Rebecca Varela
Operations manager David Scotto
Production controller Corinne Whitsun-Jones
Circulation manager Nicole Pearson
Demand forecast analyst Rebecca Williams

Published by Bauer Media Books, a division of Bauer Media Ltd,
54 Park St, Sydney; GPO Box 4088, Sydney, NSW 2001.
phone (02) 9282 8618; fax (02) 9126 3702.
www.awwcookbooks.com.au

Printed by Toppan Printing Co, China.

Australia Distributed by Network Services,
phone +61 2 9282 8777; fax +61 2 9264 3278;
networkweb@networkservicescompany.com.au
New Zealand Distributed by Netlink Distribution Company,
phone (64 9) 366 9966; ask@ndc.co.nz
South Africa Distributed by PSD Promotions,
phone (27 11) 392 6065/6/7; fax (27 11) 392 6079/80;
orders@psdprom.co.za

Title: Recipes from around the world /food director, Pamela Clark.
ISBN: 978-1-74245-279-1 (pbk.)
Notes: Includes index.
Subjects: International cooking.
Other Authors/Contributors: Clark, Pamela
Dewey Number: 641.59

Cover and chapter openers
Photographer Ian Wallace
Stylist Louise Pickford
Food preparation Sharon Kennedy
Cover Paella valenciana, page 96 and Grilled haloumi, page 36.

To order books
phone 136 116 (within Australia) or
order online at www.awwcookbooks.com.au
Send recipe enquiries to:
recipeenquiries@bauer-media.com.au